D1290120

Archaeologist of a Word…

Love Yourself
Respect Yourself
And Value Yourself

Angel Ramos

Printed in the United States of America

First Printing, 2016

ISBN: 978-1-5356-0025-5

Just the one word walk your reality

Don't be afraid to knit a word, the joy in the laugh of the smile will correct it

The power to be is just smile at everything. Everything is nothing movement. Learning of word true as being. Understanding give thinking it's true reality, word as a sentence give present its experience it's told. A page without written leave complex. A signature of sign leave simple. A hug with the experience of a smile is a perplex of life

Matter as essence
Solution as thinking
Formula as understanding
Chemistry as sentence
Combine as words
Science as smile

If one post the mirror upside-down, it will still post the horizon

The hands that touch your words is a smile

To record the sound
One must become a mirror
SILENCE REFLECTION

Read now as a sentence of a second

Essence mistakes are never...

Beginning of everything is a word
The power in the sentence of now

Center the sentence
To become a word

Pulling a tooth out a word

Body searching in a sentence

Boom, that simple

Make your stage a play-ground...

Vocabulary of the sound
Is a word in essence
The frequency of understanding
As the tone of thinking
Only present can notes its pitch

Believe, creates
Deeps truth

Pearl the silk in written

Read writing understanding Thinking

A job without function, isn't a smile
Love yourself, that's the duty

The are no obstacles, one can jump

Don't blank the essence

Create the unspoken, fore-told the un-told

The bag of water, as one pebble

Give movement an action
  Now see if it matches the smile

Sitting here, while essence moves

Don't the words be air
  The wind may write something

The parallel of the words is the form of the sentence

The portion of the smile
  Is the ingredients of the word

If essence was the ink
  And present the pen
  Plus thinking as paper
  What would understanding
  Write as now

Sign the word of now's present

I will scripture your horizon
Carry the spoken as present

The written of signature is present

To abbreviate a smile
Just become present of word

The administration of the heart, one knows it's the smile

Why does thinking don't listen to understanding

Use now as the writer of present

Stand movement is called sweet love

Why does an answer need an explanation ... toys aboard

As a child one marinated (why)
As a adult one marinated (how)
As a present one marinated (now)
As a word one marinated (self)
As a thinker one marinated (understanding)
As a essence one marinated (spirit)

Match the smile to the laughter

Make the reason of a thought

Heaven the dance floor
And baby-powder as the clouds
Works as essence sound
Off to the place call love

Simply soft, align the words

Question understanding, the will walker

If one takes thinking out of understanding
The eyes will see its presentation

Essence may walk
But understanding talk

Essence as heaven
Understanding as thinking
Words as self
Hugs as smile
Now as present
We as ONE

Action the motion
Act like a light

As a shine teaching a light

Horizon teaching the day

The truth of truth is the hidden...
Don't have a drone day
 Cyber the words as
 Input and output
 The domain in
 Engineering is the sentence
 Put that in the wallet

If an envelope was a smile, what would it say... look for the stamp 1st
B-4 answering

Understanding walk essence around in thinking, to see if everything OK

Making choices are lyrics of understanding
 Not sound of thinking

Doctor love...and nurse divine

Essence is the place where understanding teaches thinking about present
in now

Fire le smile
 Horizon the destiny
 Pour your shore
 As connection harmony
 Sprinkle words shine

The alignment of words the mirror

Kingdom of pebbles
Ocean of stream
Come lean on thy simple dream

The rebel of hugs are smiles

The vitamin of a word Is the sentence

How can one merchant a smile, word it up

Now the puddle

Why claim there

Look at the view from see, it's called language

The present in essence
Is the word in now

Clear the mirror, by correcting the sentence

Don't let tears scratch mirrors

I am the statue of a word
I am the pillar of the word

Choice has chance, look under the words. I NOSE THERE IS A SMILE

If every pages of a book are mirror, one can paragraph its story like. Words as present, understanding as truth, and thinking as am. The book would title SELF...

The pen as a tears is the ink as a smile

PRACTICE SELF-LOVE, AND WATCH PRESENT BECOME MIRROR

Use a tear as a scratch-off
And win your heart

A HEART PUMPS BLOOD, NOT TEARS

Guidance is the sentence
One make in any word

One can power any word

A cloud never follows you

Let go of the wrecking ball
Shadow a smile for present

One is the essence
As present is now
One can draw as smile
One can be as ALL
One can sign View
One can worship being

One give gifts own
The one in one as mirror

The individual in words
Is the sentence in opportunity

Smile the simple in move as silence hugs itself

Smile the indicated move

Everything is giving in a word, smile, love, shine, and even opportunities. Words can expand in to view. Words can be enlightened for joy. Words open communication between a wall n mirror, wait for it. Words can teach you say HELL 2 THE NAH

The water gravity of a sentence Is a smile

Battery is not water, so live...

Polly the book

You are in the right page
  But wrong sentence...

If life gives you a sentence, make lemonade

Talk, said the word to the sentence

As I walk in the valley of forest
  I shall fear no ocean.

ESSENCE, THE TEACHER AS UNDERSTANDING
AND STUDENT AS THINKING
PRESENT AS A PICTURE
SIMPLE THAT'S ALL...
Smiles are reflection of essence

Make a SUN, just smile walking

The spoon-full of a pill is the sentence

Don't talk what you going lie about...

Today is just simple
Just be you in words

The here as is in now
Present understanding Thinking

Always the present of is in now

Present the view-finder of a word

Present can draw your second

A smile as a walk, is a sentence as a hug

Let the ego walk

Post your smile as a hug

A book can't open its heart
Only its words CAN...

There is no time in a line
Don't limbo the words in essence

The home of the brave is the eyes of the heart

The atom of nothing
The particular of everything
How am I here in essence
Now as understanding
Is the theme of thinking
I made say vision signs
Can view ink in a pen
Present teach the wow of truth
As words draw ebony
As a pearl as ivory
And the eyes as heart

The team of a sentence
But coach by a word
Is a smile sponsor by present

I have tears with a smile
But it's memory hurts
With its understanding seed
The mirror can plant a garden reflection

A sky is the billboard of a smile

Love can fill a bucket without a sentence
Love can tell one a challenge
 If it laughs, better check the challenge

The pages of a word

Leave WHAT IS, alone

Plain is the simple of sentence

Follow, the steps in words

Understanding the pillar of thinking
 Present the universe of present
 Hugs the smile of words
 We the Is in words

Don't age words...

The sentence of a direct smile
 Makes the horizon shine over the shadow

Centeredness is found by hugs

Joy is a laugh in a smile

Read is the language of written

Don't throw tears at the heart
One may break the heart...

The science of a word
Is a sentence
Sshhhh... ESSENCE thinking as UNDERSTANDING

The essence of a word Is a smile
The gravity of a sentence Is a hug...

The law of nature
How to platform
A word or a sentence

Nothing is the QUESTION
as everything is the ANSWER
LIFE AS VERSE OF ESSENCE

The morning graphics of a word Is a smile

Now the paper of why as a pen

Action is now as a sentence

Reality is stillness movement

Debate, a class-room pointing finger

Use the heart as the backdrop of words

Am, the mirror of essence as understanding

One can chew gum and watch TV at the same time...
Now can one love words as mirror
Care for sentence as words
View thought as understanding
Draw a smiles as support
Look at thinking as essence of am
Here is the why as what

Experience as essence
Present as understanding
sign as thinking

Essence, opportunity as a sentence

Parallel

Nothing is the now present

Everything is the sentence words

Essence is understanding. Thinking
SMILE IS HUG KISSES
And horizon is light shine
See is views look
As now is why what
Reading writing as sign

Passion of a word's

Sentence of its smile
Essence become a reflection
Understanding teach think
Look as in see
Touch as in read
The horizon as love
Grace speak in present
Spoken as a hug
Time writes be
A forest as a sentence
A word as a tree
I plant the present
In the sea of smile

Definition of term is a sentence reason

Life words is a sentence
 Life word is a smile

Basic of a smile are its words

NOW, the author of a smile

Essence the paragraph of view,
 Written by see as present

Infinity essence present as NOW...

Draw the label of an ART as a smile

TIME AIN'T, let that battery in...

Use the smile as a ruler
Complex is not weave, it's only a back-pack

Word's move in a sentence, but born in a smile

Don't hatch a word in my bucket

TREAT LIKE NO-OTHER, sentence as the word

Ready for another accountability week

Good morn walking glory

Am the essence
I the understanding
Thinking the WHO
LOVE THE PRESENT
BE, THE REAL

Put here in there
And that's how IS...
THE WHAT OF WHO
the view as voice
Silence as create

I dare one view the present of theory, see can read IS...

As one walks upon an essence, PRESENT speaks

Once upon a past, ENDS present

Smile the light of a hugs
Hugs words, one's sentence

Learn the mirror
 Reflection the teacher
 Smile the student
 LIGHT THE WORD

DON'T NUMBER TIME.

Smile the guidance of time

Muah is I
 As Am is kiss

Mirror sentence as I

Remember the shadow of the word
 Is the sentence of the eyes

Look around his face he has a heart

Laying back chilling, I was born in the system.

Land is for words, not wars

THE PULSE OF A WORD IS A SMILE...

Eyes are the photos-copy of WORDS...

A place is here
 As is in now
 Present as a sentence

Pope to religion
 Socrates to philosophy
 Understanding to thinking
 SELF to WORDS
 ESSENCE to PRESENT ...

Don't be distance, to the near word...

Don't let a finger be the counselor of your words

Life is a remote, watch the finger

Cave, Republic of the teacher

Can one hear the wind in the words
 It's the sentence of the SKY...

One can't read half a word,
 If the other half is a sentence
 The balance center of present

Or the radius of essence
Is the word in LIGHT...

The add of the sum is the solution
If one understand one may think

Bullshyt week ahead, making a garden of it regardless....

The dot of life, PRESENT...

I see nothing, the start-kit
Remember one can see nothing

There going be a surprise in Fucking-A-Rite

Add sum number sounds
Toony the wave of a word
How to start a beginning,
Train a sentence...

A word is a shadow of protection,
Not a slight
Sollow of a ghost

The theory of a window is the bang of a word

BECARE-FUL OF THE WATER STEP...

COMPLETE THE BEGINNING BY SMILING

Love Yourself

Respect Yourself

And Value Yourself

FOR EVERY LAUGH IS THE SENTENCE OF A SMILE

a word has a respond called MIRROR...

Essence and music

EQUALITY essence written
As a book say
Be my present in being
I shall always shadow you
As one read light...

PRICE is what one IS...

Just is the let it be...

Movement the ending of a sentence, and beginning of the words

Start is the finish...

Love, give it a walk

I need fluid, where the music

Tears the ink of smile
Words are the light of smile
Example are free
Result are divine

In grave smile with words

My math is the music
 My equation is its smile
 With a word as a shine
 And a universe as a essence
 Understanding talk as thinking...

Smile in laughter is become

Give a menu to a sentence, become it's word...
Like a mic, it blesses words...

At the beach with my AC...
 Beach 95%
 AC remote control %
 Now make connection!!!
Let a word light your week like a sentence

Out there in the essence feeding spirit

Love don't leave your spirit without it...yeaaaababy

Music is the bite is LOVE

Me be like in H♥E♥A♥R♥T...

Marriage is not a divorce-court...

Don't push an envelope, when no answer...

Essence the experience of life

Smile the reader of it

Experience, experience by signing nothing

Strong in essence
As I create understanding
Thinking has illusion
Thoughts have dream
But decisions have position...

Words where smile are shine
And tear are emotions

Words the mother-land of thoughts
Participate the movement action
Riddle that one...

Love can be an art
If one can canvass a smile

Seconds, the books of one word...

Words starting point ending, everything beginning. Essence the paper as
understanding the pen. Before thinking becomes presents

Love become a mirror when you smiling

This galaxy note edge is no-joke

Music hangover, the shots of NOTE

The seeds of fruits
 Happy mother's day

The sum of words...

Nothing, the chance of a life....

Try to play with nothing, I bet you been doing all your. And didn't kno nothing...

Let's follow the sentence

Restore a monument of words, become the sentence of thee smile
We are all EQUAL...

One can create an apple by its seed...
 One can create LOVE by its SMILE

Essence the sentence of love in one WORD...

A sentence is the in-put of a word

Like 2 love

Page a sentence as a WORD...

Let the note lite your-life

Live in music smile

Shyt I'm Hungary and not from Europe

Never the light of nothing

Love the guidance of a sentence

A star is not a bright star, but a firm smile

Who-ever is playing at prepartradio now is smoking...WERK-QUE

Need of necessary,
 AM of wanted...

If I had to move a smile, I would start with present as it end in a hug...

JUST...

Why people request me to a game, request me to a bar. I don't drink...
you will WIN...

My boss don't like noise at work, so I brought a wireless blue- speaker

Thanks for the true love of mirror...
As a sentence
 Represent a word
 Blessing as a given
 Wings as smile
 Thanks for the BEING...
 God gave words
 MIRROR as respond

Understanding can release thinking...

STAND, write, and be free...

Free the essence as understanding

Free the chainsaw of tears...

Feed your words, sentence…
And watch it's roots be smile...
Feed your heart, hugs
And watch its core be ESSENCE

One smile is the billboard of a sentence

Love write you everything as a smile

A sentence is a bucket of a words

One can fold a word into a sentence, JUST sMiLe

Patience in waiting
Present in silence
The heard in action
MOVEMENT SPEAKING
The what of why...

Essence is the conductor
As the transformer is understanding...
Enlighting the light

Present the block-board of a smile...

Correct what's good for one...Self

One can't make honey with-out sugar
 Simple buy a bed...

The origin of a smile is its WORDS...
 The laugh are its signature...
 The light of essence

Muah said to self...

Cloud may be dark, but can't cover SHINE...

Walk action movement...

Nothing, but something shine...

HELP, said the worry word...

Music has a playground the SMILE

Beginning is holding an ending

Map are not on the EYES, there in the smiles

Out of range
 No radar
 Center closed

Go find another bodega
How to open words

Closed-mind
Shut-window
Think-upsidedown

Meaning understanding is reason thinking...ARTI-choke

The so-called many curve-light SELF

Blessing for every second as a sentence

Be real, or be page...

One can build kingdom on water, turning tears into smile...

RESULTS are CARING

Words are the impact of a smile...

Zombie, no thank-you. 12th step...

The sum of one are three, just point...

Rhetoric of psalm are relic of scripture. Un-weave the sentence of a word.
Or tide the to a sentence as a smile

Be nice...

The wind sing
 Song dance

Take the jacket of that smile...

Natural philosophy is a SMILE

Note words as smile...

To pour music to the cup of the HEART...

quantum theory
 mythology prophecy
 how can one think in words
 >>>>>>> understanding<<<<<<<

To be words
 One must study AM
 Simple am is the mirror

Train a word
 Become it's SMILE...
 :-))

A light contribute to a smile
 A sentence contribute to a words

Write what is written
 A light in the dark
 Essence as thinking

Understanding as words
Believe as creation
The AM of self

Smile, the words that fit right into a sentence...

Glass of mirror
Words of essence
Understanding of thinking

A smile the light of cement

One be as the universe IS...ONE
Practice the polishing

Words could be written in a book, but only live in a smile

the way to fit in is a sentence...

Create a sentence as a smile

The gate-way of love is a smile

Don't make the media a mirror…

Once upon a time, the end called nothing

Color truth in understanding called words

Thinking might give one the universe, but understanding will give one its atom

Thinking with-out understanding
It's like saying batteries not included...

Why a goal, if it's not a WORD

Dear you, I say thank you for AM...
SELF

The body is the pencil of words call action vision in present

I fell over thinking, but I'm in love with understanding...
Essence the believe in words

Opinion, need I say no-mas...

Be a second, don't give it TIME

Essence is written, just hear the word AM. In every understanding

If war nothing, then why point...

One can draw a smile with a Hug

Distance is nowhere
As here is always

Not to the right-side

Not to the left-side
Only balance can tell one the truth

Guide of words
Scripture of smile
Understanding of thinking
The blessing of hugs

To sign a sky
Use the eyes as a smile

The contract of words is a smile

Tears the story's of emotion
Smile the story's of joy

Like tears if one look into there are smile

Essence the looking-glass of words

The mirror
The book
The question
The answer
The thinking
The understanding
Essence creates believe
Spirit creates smile

Crazy how smile serve tears

movement stands still, only vision can see it's action

you can't STOP stillness

Listen works in a one-way

Life so funny as a blank...

Why a boss wear, a hat when thy is a _____!!! Three strike and Thee will be mys...

Don't sell ticket, if one hiding tooth...

The stamp of a smile are words

Give tears a jump-rope, to find the smile

Inside the book of SMILE, there are scripture writing by smile

HERE I AM...pow

Smile the born of words...

The world is BTFUL,
  Don't write it with a TEAR...

Tears the ink of a smile

Sound carry the lyric

One can pull a tooth if one a mirror

If one can hold water like one says, make sure is Ice

Funny how the teeth talk, but the tongue LIES

You WON a free around the world
 You can start walking anytime you want...

SCRATCH-OFF ARE NOT COPYS

Push the wig back, by pulling the tooth… essence TRUTH > > ;-))

What is the question
 As why is the question

Paint the sentence of the day
 By being the art-word of the night

There is no purpose in still...

Don't let a tear, rain on a sentence...

Connect to your world, and the world will be the same...always IS of Now

Selfish is not an intuition

One can be a mirror without words...

Don't rain on a smile

A tear can't hear a smile

Words shine, the understanding control of smile saying

Only u can lead words

In a trail of a sentence, there is a balance called always in words

Days are the LIFE
 NIGHT are the PAGES

In every word is a smile, just make it in understanding. And be it as Born

Need humor make a softly with a heart

I'm loading a smile at work...

Give the secret expression of present

I am note of sound called SMILE

Love the stand of a smile

Words can draw tears, but pillar smile

My shoulder can take no-more

Thought diverse decision into everything. When's how for WHY love sign days in smile...

my smile feel like
a surf-board in the sky

Have you listen to your EYES...

Words are the only church of sentence

The vision is silence
The sentence one give it

Soft is the smile, that has the garden of words

If the wallet don't fit the shoe, change IT. Words of the tree, that fell far from the apple, orange, and banana...

Only words peak by sound
Made by sentence

For is one to love
Love must care
Words said by words

Love is real, a lifesaver candy isn't

Love is a shore in reach...

Ask a word a joke, but be careful of its laughter

For all the love, there is only one smile "truth"

Two roses walk into a bar...

AND THEN ONE...

THE ART OF a SMILE IS TO WORD IT, the sign signature of ESSENCE

The ART of a WORD,
  Draw the story of the SMILE

The flow of beauty is written in silent words

One can't give a smile a sentence
  It has. Chapter of its own. Words made of sentence, as essence SPEAK

CAUTION, no sitting on BRAIN... it bad for the smile...

What happen beyond close door, darkness action

Music, check
  Boat, check
  Night, check
  Dance, check
  Happy, check

IT'S O.K.

Gonna paint the town MUSIC, this weekend… treadin' glory with grace in harmony

If love is a cane
 It would lean against a HUG…

A word is a word, until one apply a smile…

Living never survive, when it contain smile

Peel an union means EMOTION
 Polish a shine reason of SMILES

Ssh secret it ain't hard is be a smile, just look at the reflection of the HEART…

Knit a weave, just smile. Complex to perplex

A word is loud, only self can hear it…spoken essence

Religion gangster hand-sign is the basket

In a land faraway call work…

The light that walk in the dark

Get your zookeeper it's raining MEOW n WOOF

Love it is, what it IS. Don't add choices to IT…

HERE is the forum of love...

a sentence, the position of a thought

love happens to everyone, because you are it...

Complain, the search product of emotion. Near at a selves near words

Tears never bleed
They only smile

No-value is expensive, tears don't have anchors

One don't hear
As one walks in the shadow
One can see in the shine

news-flash love one another as words connecting
a sentence bondin is a smiling mirror

how can you read the fog
when your eyes are the trees

Of one can catch a tear...

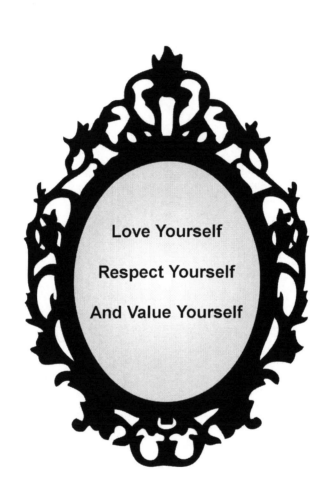

Love Yourself

Respect Yourself

And Value Yourself

One just caught the world...

WISE DONT FIT, let it sink

Walk a shine as one is the shadow...reflection of an echoes

Hear what is love of action, to be what is understanding of movement... creation essence heard

Open the sentence to dance on the word...

every word is the mirror of now...

If you can count up to three in silence, and hear it. You just became essence. The mirror in the echoes is the light in the heart...

The bread-crumb word is the planted seed...

Be the sentence of the glass, that a mirror...

Show me a meeting, and -
  I'll show you a body...

Start love with a begin...

A second is the start of anything everything all thee TIME...

Simple your smile with words, you are their guidance, teacher, and student

Words say hello in SELF...

One can walk a line, the guildin' sentence...

Find self in viewin' words... the present of vision

Don't block a sentence,
 Or one can't fine the word

LOVE CENTER EVERY WORD, THAT THE THINKING MAKES EMOTION

CENTER, A SPOT OR DOT, WHERE A SQUARE TRIES TO GET INTO

Going on a venture called YOGA...

Voices in my head are singing LOVE SANG...

Love the burp of believe...

essence decision thought
 thinking, understanding believe

Get off the cream-cheese, if you can't bake a WORD...

THE MOMENT...think now, are you applyin' understanding

Brian it out...

ROW-CALL, SELF

ALERT, love thy SELF

Words are the only thing that breathe and see!!!

Love is the only chain-ball, enlighten by the HEART...

If love is art
 Then a smile a painting

The bridge of a word
 Is the words of understanding sentence

The greatest word ever TOLD...LOVE

The mirror of today word is share...

A word that's a universe... SMILE

To have and to hold, WHAT A SMILE WOULD Say

Open the day in a word...and the night will rest in a sentence

Road-trip, MTA to central-park...iron horse therapy

Get off, it's not your stop...

Funny how the HAVES , can't fit threw a wide DOOR

Black or white
Decision or thought
Yes or No
Big bang theory
Fractals myth
Strings complex
Perplex LOVE
Essence divine
Self AM in I
ALL believe creation
UP or down
True or false
Moments Quality
Passion wonder
With open smile
There is a HUGS...

Imagine that, I heard you SAY...

Understanding can be the teacher
Now can one be the thinking
The essence of words
One can help words by becoming their UNDERSTANDIng

Measurin'-tape, stop blamin' what AIN'T...

The chapter of a paragraph is the giving words of sentence

A smile parallel any sentence

A smile is not a cape, it's an umbrella

A smile has no weight, only words

Pasts lighten future PRESENT

A shadow holds secrets

LOVE WILL ALWAYS TELL...

Rain pisses people off, cause there no SHINE...
WORDS pisses people off, cause there no UNDERSTANDING

LIFE and LOVE
BODY and ESSENCE
Which one 1st
The tree or the egg

If love is a mirror, that's ones reflection

Read into IS, and find what the AM is in I...

The wind won't say what the words EXPLAIN...

Love stand where ever one At

Ask each word
Thank you for your shadow

LAUGH, THE PILLARS OF SMILE, LOVE REASON

LOVE WAVE IS A SMILE, SO BRING THE SHORE OF SHOULDERS...

I DON'T HAVE NOTHING THAT I WANT, BUT GOT EVERYTHING THAT I AM...

ONE CAN SELF FAVOR WORDS

Situation are control by SELF

Difference in same, mirror, always and Now
Study the word SAME...

FOCUS AWARENESS, NOW MOVEMENT AND STILLNESS ACTION

AND I SAID IT, ...self

The element of LOVE is SMILE

Love follow you in shadow, but make it to PRESENT...

if one put an empty cup of water in the brain, one will still drown...geee

don't carry words on your shoulder, let them be shadow

PRICES WHAT VALUE, I say words

Love SIZE everything...

It never takes long to become A smile

Smile the ladder of the straight walk

Who can say NO to music…heck-with-No

The Heart will be there complete for smile

The heart write every sentence of the SMILE

Every word has a written sentence in it called REASON

THE LINE OF A HOUSE IS A SMILE

Even in the rain-forest TEARS
 The branches fruit SHINE

The particular article in words is SELF

BE MY GUESS, HUMBLE THE UNDERSTANDING

Essence is like a bucket
 Thinking made be it's water
 Understanding is its real taste
 But words is the real mirror of the glass

Read the story of the eyes, there are TWO, but only see present

WALK a distance in a present word…NOW!!!

IF LOVE CAN WEAVE A WAVE
A SMILE CAN CURVE A SENTENCE

Don't burn the bridge of a sentence, it become the cliff of a word path

STRUCTURE YOUR ESSENCE
BLUE-PRINT OF SELF

SMILE THE TEACHER
LOVE THE STUDENT

TEARS THE AWAKEN TABLET

Tears help if one listen, don't por aways your answer

NOTHING MIST, the product of a sentence

DON'T BE A SHADOW OF A WORD, BE ITS PURPOSE...sponsor by a SMILE

A word is the teacher of a sentence

A sentence is the shadow of a word

Only words can lead a sentence

The light in the heart give rays

The lotus of a rock
The smile in a ROSE

We all stand------

The forest in the water-fall sings every Now

The pen of a tears
 Writes the painting of a smile

No poetry, or philosophy
 Can be the mirror of a smile

THE EYES OF A SENTENCE ARE TEARS AND SMILE

Same in a sentence, as the one word in a mirror

Many tears for the perfect smile
 A river crossing
 A bridge walked
 A journey gift
 For one is the made in made
 As the one in art painting

The current of flower
 Is the shine of its smile

Silk the pearl of a smile, or the shine of a word

SMILE the full of a word

LAUGH IS MADE OUT THE SENTENCE OF A SMILE...

A ROSE HAS BEAUTY
 BUT its SMILE IS COURAGE

Blue can be read
 As shown in red
 But white can see the truth black...the color of shine

An inch is deep-far in tears

Chapter of love
 Blessing of words
 Giving of smile

If I write in the air
 How can wind read the words
 Oh yea cause the trees are singing it...

IS, the quality of BORN

Love can fill with THINKING
 ESSENCE can be fill with UNDERstanding

If love was a runner, its mile would be a second

Love don't have instruction, is an essence of present

FOR WHERE THERE IS LOVE, THERE IS ALWAYS SELF IN WHERE...

HI, there words...

Like or now, it IS...

Present will tell you the whole story

Seconds the teacher of moments

The height of understanding is the straight dotted line

The only FLAG in words are smile

You can't staple a word in a smile, by licking it...

WORDS don't have nails...

TEARS the damp rag...

WATER CAN BE A TOWEL...

EGO, mirror's with battery...

WAIT FOR IT, SHYT JUST PAST

For one that mirror, words of present

Science and art of a smile, a word and its REASON for PRESENT

Don't reap the weave of a complex tears, the smile eraser

The words are the blue prints
The sentence are the bricks
Thinking are the building
And understanding are the pillar
Smile are the complete picture

Don't claim the sentence, if thy words are empty

An atom in a word, a bucket of understanding. Or an emotion a cup of thinking. Weight in tear

If a water-drop can break a rock in half, DONT LET A TEAR BREAK A HEART INTO PIECES...

THESIS THEORY, a smile MAKING...

Solutions weave is the sentence of one word, breaking a thought in one's decision

A word platform is a MIRROR

The replica of repeat is a MIRROR

For one-love is a MIRROR, reflection the echoes silence

The gatherin' of the mass is the sentence of one WORD, understanding teachin' thinkin' essence

Thinking will start, when understanding READY

Understanding giving a 5minute timeout to thinking

The doctor words, made the sentence be the smile

Love is not to be wet with TEARS...is to be shine with a smile

GRAVITY CARGO, the smile

If nothing has a compliment, accept IT...heart emoticon

MUAH for the REACH...

The motivational speaker of words is understanding silence in heard

THE BALLAD OF WORDS IS A SMILE...

The action in truth is understanding

WHY IS TO THE POINT ANSWER, Not question

TOMORROW WORDS IS TODAY UNDERSTANDING OF YES-TERDAY THINKING

POUR YOUR-SELF A SMILE...

INVEST IN SMILE NOT TEARS, where the sugar shine

Chances by choice...at a word near YOU!!!!

How u like self NOW

HOLD me ask WORDS

Don't let the current be a TEARS, said the wave

To find the answer in WHY As IS...

GO under to see what's beyond

For one is in AM, the mirror of self

My community is the foundation of a sentence, that builds pillar words

A word with-out a smile is damage-good

FOR-EVER LOG-ON A SMILE...

The measure of time, as a smile
 Is the art of the painting
 Or the word of the sentence
 Understanding is the math in thinking
 Smile is the time-table of WORDS

A sound of a voices is the essence in the heart
 The call of a decision in a thought
 Movement talks in its silence
 The heard of moment in NOW
 Or the secret of second as sentence
 The voices of a word in silence

IS understanding teachin' thinkin'
To be a student and to GROW as a SMILE
The water of a smile can share experience
The light of a mirror can be the echoes of reflection
AS same in all is ONE
A word repeats in CARING...

The experience that could've BEEN...

A stream is part of an ocean
 Essence part of the heart
A smile is part of a HUG

A smile the shovel of emotions

A smile is a log on the ocean, not a ROCK

Follow the beginning of a smile, it will find its own ending

Light the sentence of a smile

A smile never has garbage

A wall melts with a smile...

Movement ain't a thought, it's a beginning

Understanding ain't got nothing to with strong, or power. It have to do
with what's right, and be careful with that one TOO...

A word can travel in walk
AS it's does in movement

A word that stand, reads a lot...

SIMPLE, the IS...

SMILE, the guide in LIFE...

Where in IS, there is UPON

STILL TEACHIN SILENCE,
Hearin' vision as heard
READIN' TALK

CLIMB NON-MOVEMENT...

The reason I reason is UNDERSTANDIN, property of THINKING...

YOU ME RIGHT, LOVE THING...

The step was done, before the height

a smile only ask for btful words to be itself...

Love don't scare, it only laugh...

Music is the way I live
I alive and living NOW
From the day I was BORN...

We have a word, said the sentence

We have a decision said the thought

We have a smile said the HUG

We have a understanding said the thinking

We have a essence said the SPIRIT

We have a WE said the mirror

One push a shovel, one gain a COLD. Where is the karma in that...2/17/14

It's better to shovel in the summer, jus' me saying

MAKE AM INTO EVERY WORD!!!!!

The switch of life in understanding...

Believe is the building-block of thinking

AS essence is the picture

Smile will be the TRUTH

SELF the MIRROR of ALL

WE, the challenge of a sentence. Written as one WORD...

ARE is IS, IS Is ARE.

The am as I in SELFTHOUGHTS, CREATER OF ONES DECISION. THE MASTER OF A SIMPLE WORD. Be careful don't drown now. Awareness-focus

Sign a smile as a signature, AM control the thought or decision

MIRROR, your heart as a paper and pen, the sentence will create. What is born in smile

Deep in the sentence of gold, a smile is pour, shine as a pearl. The word walks in present

One word told the other word, hold my hand and unite thee in a smile. So the reflection can be the mirror

Ones blessin' is the sentence in the other heart... the mirror smile in word

The wheel of technology is down-loadin'
The wheel of thinking is understandin'
The wheel of smile is a hug
The wheel of love is believe
The wheel of essence are words

The voice the tears in my heart, thanking everybody blessin' giving to me

CONSULTING: thinking the student
Understanding the teacher
Essence the Answer
LOVE the question
Being the Smile...

Today a child was born, the three wise left three present, a smile, a hug, and the middle finger...and said happy birthday u brat hahahahaha

If one can smile, buildin' a sentence

If one can create nothing

Imagine the power one has

Don't let feather break MIRROR

Even water has FIRE...

Like the record says, YOU DON'T KNOW...

Treat SELF says The word

Out of work and on full-force, on the the powder floor week...

FOR WHOM COVER, LIGHT UPON...

For thy is the reach of thee, LE SMILE

For each thought is a sentence, for each smile is a WORD

A word is the description, a sentence is the BELIEVE

EMOTION IS THE RECORD THAT NEVER HAS THE RIGHT
VOLUME

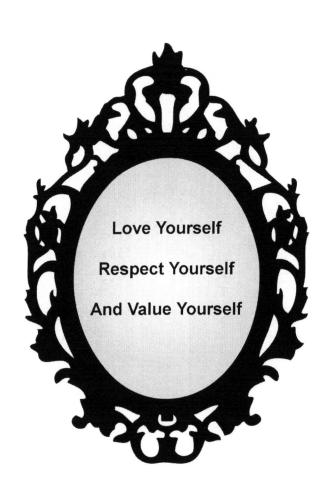

Love Yourself

Respect Yourself

And Value Yourself

AS one walks into the valley of a smile
Sentence are the trees of forest
AS the wind blow, the essence sing it's SONG
AS the foot-print of harmony
The told TALES of love is heard...

DRY WATER TO CHECK

Reason isn't for its meaning, it's for it SMILE

Drop and move, silence sentence

Ocean of emotion, put it on a shelf. Until thirsty to smile

Cover everything with self, but remember some water is not solid...

Enjoy the paradox of a word, become their sentence

ESSENCE, the power of THINKING in UNDERSTANDING
The muster seed of a TREE is a SMILE
The map of distance is a HUG...
The magic of illusion is BELIEVE
The word of a sentence are the pillar of a forest

ESSENCE CAN WRITE A SENTENCE
IF CAN READ THE SMILE

A SMILE IN SILENCE
PRINTS A HUG IN PRESENT...

Any word is a dragon, if one set the right FIRE...essence the light

Smile is just not a pearl, it's a reflection in the eyes

Walk a smile, let the dotted line be the SENTENCE...

Pillar the strength as sentence

Smile the furfill of tears

A mistake is an opportunity...

The right of wrong is correction

DON'T BE THE MEANING, BE THE REASON...

VERSUS are the same, think of understandin'. Boom there you go

Tears the glass-pages of MIRROR, SMILE are SENTENCE

Understandin is the water AM walks on, said the words of pillar

UNDERSTANDING OPEN the language of THINKING, the calling of ESSENCE as heard in HEAR. Vision speaker in silence. The pitch of volume in words

The step in the book of words, is the foot-print in understand. A word say all in your understanding, not of its meaning

ONES, TWO-WAY. Thinking UNDERSTANDIN'

Rain in the light...

IS, PAI'S paradox....

Words believe them in understandin'
Create them in lovin'
Action them in smile
Bless them in LAUGH...

FRUITS...any hint

Find a smile in the words, because is you....

All everything is self

Love injection, the smile

On the light for ME...

Don't start your TIME with your EYES, the mirror in the HEART
ESSENCE

REFLECTION of a SMILE
MIRROR of WORDS
VISION in ESSENCE

Signature the smile of a PAGE...

The unity of a smile is the true sentence of a mirror

The weight of love, is a feather of a smile

Leave the body
And bring the SOUL
MUSIC is my SONG

Muahh to my world in words call YALL!!!!

Taught of told, the singing mirror

Tears are the teaching mirror, of the student smile

If you walk a second, you will have a present

Be careful even ugly has a smile

Why design the color of bullshyt in thought...

A smile is not a reward, it's a reflection...

The tea of smile are tears...

If you btful, and I'm btful. Why are we different, question ask AN-
SWER...

Battle ground, come on SNOW...
Read as the rainbow
Write as the ribbon

Ready for hecules with salt...

Sentence can make the WORD, now are the words correct in sentence as present...self everythin' in the am of nothing

Start begin in END...the present of sentence in one pillar WORD!!

Read as the rainbow
 Write as the ribbon

Always the picture of AM, I as the reflection...

Always the never...understand the one out

to polish my drink in words...thirst quench in ESSENCE

If candy is a smile, then I AM the factory...

A word is a GIFT, and its glory is the action...:-♥
SAY THE WORDS IN UNDERSTANDIN'

The shield and a sword
 The word with its sentence...

Perfect moment always the same as now!!!!!

A mirror is walking says words, a echoes shine

Silence the fill of words, listen become learn

THE CREATER OF A SMILE IS A SENTENCE

LOVE THE ESSENCE AS AIR IN BELIEVE

WHY, WHEN ARE. MIRROR SAY...

LOVE PROTECTS FROM EMOTION OCEAN TEAR

UNDERSTANDIN'. LOVE
THINKIN' CREATION

Walkin' in thought is the decision

HISTORY, PRESENT SAME. That never change

A SMILE LANGUAGE IS A TEAR THAT SEE BEAUTY

The water of words

Said the heart to the smile

ONLY stand as UNDERSTANDIN, bridge that stand

Get off my plateau of the sand-grain

Muah of Words

In tears love search for smile...

Judgement are the tears, that full with joy...

Music in the vein is the smile in the HEART...

What words SAY!!!!

To sign smile, signature UNDERSTANDING

A violin has hidden silence
 AS words in smile

Spirit, you color it with a smile
 You print it with a sentence
 And you live it with a WORD

The inner-diamond of a flower is a smile

Mother-nature, COFFEE hahaha

Understandin' TOLD thinkin'

Love ask!!!!

Time is always the same even After YEARS...only present

Can one define the signature of words, smile it IS

By LETTING WORDS LOVE...

The remedy of smile are words...

My little cave at work with subwoofer...can anybody say FiREhahahaa

Control the words, become its understanding

Peacefully Stop the Wars...

A scripture is a sentence hidden in a words, told by silence in vision

Silent will dry any rain
 Smile will out-shine any emotion
 Laughter the brick-layer of WORDS

Only the smile can give the story of TEARS...

The mirror has an author called the smile...

In the sky
 Close as a rock
 Believe is a word
 Bridges of earth
 Sentence of smile...

If one see words in vision, can one see the smile in its sentence...

Vision the inner door of words, the eyes QUEST...

The heart is the scripture in any word

GO beyond above, as in smile

Point to your nose, so you truly understand who really point-ING

There are words, and there are smile. Connect the dot as words as shine...

LIKE IS THE SHARE OF PRESENTS...

Understanding the umbrella of the HEART, when it rain emotions

Thinking said where is the understanding, words explain they are in the ESSENCE Heart

UNDERSTANDING the foot-print of THINKING

UNDERSTANDING. THE VOICE OF SILENCE...

Understanding teaches thinking how to speak…

Give is givin' in smile by laugh...

Love can't hide present...

Making noise at work, us house need ESSENCE

Sweet the words in present

Ready passed in now

Nothing the start of each word

LOVE maze of a smile are its WORDS...

Biology is the chemistry in science, love is the nature in words...the understanding in thinking presence

Everything fill words in sentence, the giving in words

Play with nothing, y'all will find the missin

Glad is a smile with words...

If a book were ones DOOR, ESSENCE Would be the key...

A drop of a sentence is the word of your scripture

The blessin' of a smile is knowin' the sentence you made of it...

SUPER DIVINE UNDERSTANDIN' WHO YOUR SMILE IS

GRACE OF A SMILE IS THE SENTENCE TRUTH...

BEAUTY IS FOR ONE WALKS IN HARMONY.

THE ELOQUENCE OF ESSENCE IS THE HUMBLE IN SMILE...

ONLY ONE WORD FIT INTO THE WHOLE HEART, AND IT IS A SENTENCE

MUAHH EVEN GIVES PRESENT...

SMILE IS A WORD, SELF MOVEMENT ACTION IN SILENCE

PRESENT IS CLEAR THE MODELS OF WORDS

simple perplex...

smooth-roar
 smile-tear

picture smile
 paint mirror

love self for bein' self...

deep in the meadow...surface begin

Actin' as if at work

I was the CEO of my FEAR...
NOW I am the child of my smile

PRESENT, THE MOVEMENT IN WORDS
 ESSENCE, THE ACTION IN SMILE
 LOVE, THE BELIEVE AS AM
 BEAUTY, MAGIC IN BLESSIN...

your surrounding is not a calendar, date, or time...IS YOUR SMILE tomorrow will bring you yesterday, cause it's always there

The remote of a thought is the decision of the toys...warning!!! toys of words can burn

An EGO can be choose by understanding...

Can smile can be balance by the side one TAKE...

One can define LOVE structure in a sentence, just page the thought and sign the decision...

FEED WORDS LIGHTS CURRENT...

THE LINE OF PURPOSE IS A JOURNEY SMILE

1ST THE SMILE, AND 2ND THE 1ST...NOWS SAME

SIMPLE WILL WIN OVER BETTER...heart emoticon - {-8

the future can talk to the past, just remember what you forgot...

ONLY A SENTENCE CAN TALK TO A WORD, QUESTION ANSWER

A SKY DRAWS
AS THE MOON PAINT
ESSENCE LOVIN
GIVIN PRESENT
REFLECT BEAUTY

SMILE SHARE
ANCHOR LAUGHTER
CRY NEEDED
HUGS COMFROT
LIGHTS SHINE UPON
CARING MIRROR STORY

EVEN THE SQUARE OF SENTENCE, HAS ITS CIRCLE WORDS

A SMILE WILL RADIUS THE MERITS

DON'T CRY IF DISTANCE IS FAR SHORE
THE WAVE WILL FIND ITS CLOSENESS

Can two iron plate bake a smile

Don't leave a blank on thy smile, thee laugh it out

The border of the TRUTH is that one lie...

Laugh fit into a smile, just ask the heart...

Love is a shake-and-bake product of words...

LOVE IS DONE...

The fundamental of a smile is the heart present...

Present is the inner-layer of the outer-layer as in NOW...

There no re-run in seconds...

Status your smile in words...

Smile have no-limits, only the heart know...

There no-volume to BIG

Milk as in work...

How can grown people have the status of a kid, really

Love is laughter, the author of a smile...

THE COMPUTER IS THE EYES OF THE UNIVERSE, SO DATA
THE WORDS AS THEE OF AM

FERTILIZE BULLSHYT WITH A SMILE...

FREE IS THE SENTENCE SMILE...

THINK AS VIEW
 LOOK AS UNDERSTANDING
 AN BELIEVE AS SMILE
 THE AM AS WORDS...

LOVE IS THE GARDEN OF A SMILE

JUST AS A PLANET IS QUIET FROM A DISTANCE
 ITS INNER CLOSENESS HAS SILENCE WORDS...

IF EVOLUTION IS LAUGHTER, ESSENCE US AS IT'S SMILE...

REMEMBER, PART OF AN HALF IS THE WHOLE TRUTH OF THE MAYBE BALANCE

BELIEVE IS A PILLAR OF WORDS, AS UNDERSTANDING IS AN ILUSION OF SENTENCE. IS A SMILE TRUTH OR A CRY PART OF EVOLUTION...

if a word is an atom, the sentence is the universe. as believe is to essence, understanding is to thinking...

a word must understand to think, essence silence express

universe the picture of essence, decorated by words...

a smile is walkin' in a thought
lookin' the the path in decision
it ask believing are the shine
everything in understanding
give thinkin' wonder beauty
then it made a decision in thought
to shine in believing
thinking as understanding
will the shine be in walk...

essence the light as understandin'
a thought in a decision
is a word in believing

DON'T LET THE SMILE BOUNCE...

ESSENCE IS EVERYWHERE IN NOTHING...JUST FILL THE BLANK

ONLY THE HEART IS THE SOIL OF THE SMILE...

WATER CAN BE HEART IN TEARS...

TEARS THE GLASS SILENCE, ONLY HEARD CAN MIRROR...

FORGOTTEN NOTHING IS TIME ALL...

FOR EVERY MEASURE DISTANCE, SILENCE BEGINNING IS NOW ALWAY IS...

FILM A SMILE, PROJECT THE WORDS...

A CRITICAL BATTERY IS AN EMOTION...

NOTHING HAS ANSWER, THAT QUESTION EVERYTHING...

SIMPLE DOES, WHAT AIN'T IS...

Love is written in smile, and read in laughter

A look, is a word that defines

Just as the sun shine on the world, one can make shine on them...
Emotion is like a wink, only one can take the tree out the light

Every word one walk in is a street, only one can light them...

LIGHT the smile as it's true Best

Rememberin' a memory, searchin' in light...

SHELTER words with SMILES...

Love is here and always support u, now can one support the mirror

Love need one comfort, so jus smile...

Love distance is a smile away...

Love opportunity is a smile...

The volume of a word is the smile...

If the thought don't have a smile, the decision can WAIT

Don't let emotion travel in smile...

The record of a word are the scratches of it's TRUTH...

Bubble the thought, by soaping the decision

Laughter can mirror, if the smile SHINE...

By written a smile, see if the words are TRUE

Teach ones smile to talk...

Only your heart is the newspaper of your SMILE...

To describe a decision, view heard...

Water, what can it tell one about the ocean and the streams

+++++++++++++++++++
smile emoticon L heart emoticon O heart emoticon R heart emoticon D smile emoticon

L EARNNING
O N
R EALITY
D REAM

if dream a thought, please believe the smile...
the HIGH in low is the converted smile...

A light ask a lantern together we make ONE, understanding told thinking. Hold my words as we make this sentence. For guidance of bless, let's comfort this journey. Will pillar the smile, in the tunnel needed light. Smile as thinkin', laughter as understanding.we will walk the dark sentence with the smile as our LIGHT...

SILENCE WILL TEACH QUIET, HOW TO SPEAK IN LISTEN...

For every become that has been...

If a sky reflects a smile, the sentence become the heart...

Every glass has a sentence
True mirror are reflection of words, that answer the question "who am i"

What is richer than laugh, ash the smile...

If one can't see a smile in a word, why call it a word...

VIEW, the universe in a WORD...if one think the universe is not in a words, ask why does it has a sentence...¡♥ :-))

Status what the smile look for in the HEART...

There is no lost in nothing...

WHY, why instead of AM...

Walkin' the smile in pillar heart...

The deck without card jus the heart...

if one can teach thinking to talk
    understanding can teach it to listen

The reader said WHY...

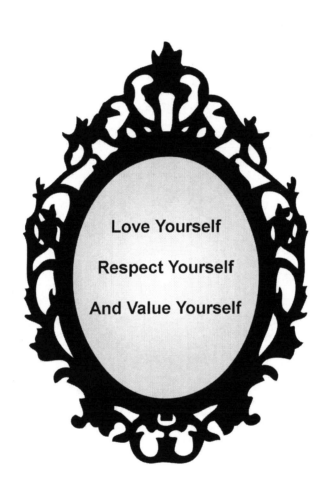

Love Yourself

Respect Yourself

And Value Yourself

WE AS THY IS THOU IN AM. The thee in SELF

ECHOE MIRROR REFLECTION, words undertandin' as ESSENCE PRESENT...

ESSENCE WRITTEN IN THE WING CALLED THE SONG...

The universe in one word is the everything of nothing. Nothing the beginning of one-words made into a sentence called the believe of UNDERSTANDIN'...

Maintain essence draw the understanding of presents...

The future is the harvest, if one plant the PRESENTS

What stay moves in silence...

The land-mine of laugh are the wallet smile...

The off-spring of words are smiles

The same as there is always the pillar of now, now, now no wait I just pass it, no wait there it is now, now now now now...

DRAW PRESENT A HEART...

BALANCE IS ONLY ONE WORD...SMILE

One can measure pain, but can't level a smile...

Why walk a journey that's still, jus live it. SPONSOR by a smile...

Desting the beginning of everything called believe...

In the woods of noise, you can hear the quiet smile...

The one's in WE, is SELF...

One can't water a forest in a dream, but one can nurture a garden in believe...

How can you carry a smile, if the heart heavy...ANCHOR LOVE

Love the sound of self in AM

Even illusion has a SMILE...buildin' foundation in essence

Time is always, the writer of now...

If time your page, SIGN IT...authors BELIEVE

In nothing everything begin...

IF SAME IS ALWAYS, THEN STILLNESS IS MOVEMENT IN SILENCE...

SMILES THE LIGHT OF SECONDS...

THE TWO-SIDE OF REACH ARE SMILE BRIDGE...

SMILE THE LOVE CENTER...
THE RE-CONSTRUCTION FOR EMOTION, ARE THE BLUE-PRINT OF SMILE

A SMILE IS THE GIFT OF EVERYTHING...

one can give everything in a simple smile...

A SMILE THE INK OF LIFE...

DON'T FORGET NOTHING, IT'S THE SOURCE OF EVERY-THING...

Some many words, for no-EAR...

Love the support of words...simples complex

Guidance by guide, reflection see mirror. The caller of light...

Deep is the word, above is the sentence...

A light can walk the path, if you become its sentence...

The foundation of a light is a smile...

Only words move you, the reflection of light...

If it is in this universe, it is a light...

Light the word called everything...

Myth, words with missing HEART...

Sign the words in HEART theory...

Said the words to thoughts...

Laughing the opportunity of life...

A pillar is a sentence of understanding. Understanding are the words of thinking. Thinking is a sentence of essence present...just take a moments it will sink IN...

One can say HI with a smile, if it's truth...

Thinking the bottom-less bliss, understanding the life-saver CANDY. Drop one in the emotions...the silver linen

The toss of nothing, the grain of darkness. The mountain of a shadow bliss. An emotion filter by the ghost of a sentence. Now are those words empty or fill. Is it a big bang theory of a fracter or fact of non-believe...

Understanding will circle a square...

Understanding is the learning of teaching...

One understanding would put thought in its place...

Hate the chain-n-ball of emotions...

A mirror is the page sign by loving words...

I know everything about NOBODY...

Shadow the reminder of self guidance...

AM the GUIDANCE , AM the WORDS

May smile be bless as words are present...

Love things like this...

CONSCIOUS AWARENESS IS THINKING UNDERSTANDING

You, anythin' else is an option

Essence products everything...love in a smile

Share is the mirror in reflection...

A written SMILE is a written HUG...

direction are smiles...

journey may be backward, but it's forward...

blessing for wondering words, pillars smile. sentence aim...

The option of lovin' self, oppss wait a second

How a decision guide the THOUGHT...

The heart of the matter, is the words of understanding

Cast yourself into a word, and see if it become AM. Guess what they all ARE!!!!!!!

BE CAREFUL, WORDS RE-WRITE THEMSELVES UNDER-EMO-TIONS

UNDERSTANDING, THE PRINTS OF THINKING...

PRESENT THE LIBRARY OF A SMILE...

GRATITUDE THE GRACE OF A GIFT WORD...

SHINE ARE THE SMILE OF THE HEART...

MOVEMENT THE LABOTORY OF A WORD

YOU CAN GAIN EVERYTHING IN A SMILE...ESSENCE GIFT

PILLARS OF HEARTS ARE SMILING WORDS...

YOUTH THE UNDERSTANDING OF A SMILE...

FOUNTAINS ARE FOUND IN WORDS

LET YOUR DREAM BE JUST THE SMILE, IT'S THE APPLI. OF EVERYTHING THOUGHTS DECISION...

Salt and sugar, oil and water, thought and decision, believe and words, and essence and AM...inquisition

TIME TO PLAY WITH MY WALLET

I WONDER HOW MANY GAMES REQUEST I'VE NEVER SEND....

THE NATURE OF A SMILE IS THE SHINE...

HOW LOVE IN LOVE CONNECT THE SMILE...

MOVEMENT ACTION A SMLE WITHOUT THE GREAM...

FINE IN THICK IS THOUGHT...

THE WORLD COULD SEE THE UNIVERSE...
THE EYES SEE THE HEART...
AND WORDS BE BELIEVED...

OFF-LINE DELETE IN-PUT...

Install any word in your heart, and make it a mirror. Make it any word you can't think of...

I feel like a pool, drinkin' so much water...

WALLS HAVE DIRECTION, TURN AROUND...

IF THE SMILE FITS THE THOUGHT

OPINION COME IN SOFT-TISSUE TOO...
ACTION IN UNDERSTANDING, THE VOICE OF SILENCE...

even the wind in the words, share a cool breeze...

Second day at makin' donut, humid the baker said to the sun...

Testin' a nerves volume...silent out loud

Comments are RARE, so this POST...

Post a smile in a sentence...

When you ever, just ever...

VENTURIN A triumph

Blank, nothings present...

Enlightenment is the words of believin' in AM...

Words mirror of AM, understandin' essence present

Wiki-dictionary, words of understanding truth...

now, back-forward present...reading action

The anchor heart, walks the smile

Walking with essence and make sure the words are there...

Let the coin of the thought, be the decision of smile...

Don't let the eyes be the hair in one tongue

Hear the quality in words...

In silence hear is heard...

For every word, there is a silence action...

EVER SEEN A WORD THINKING, JUST LOOK AT UNDER-STANDIN'

THE ENVELOPE OF WORDS IS THINKING UNDERSTAND-ING

THE JOY OF ANY WORD, IS THE SMILE ONE GIVES IT...

Words can walk on water, jus smile in the rain...

Polish the mirror with reflection

Even walls has soil, the love within

A smile is just a sentence away, that just pass one in NOW...how to center present, one don't is just IS

NOTHING MADE INTO A LIGHT...big bang sneeze

SHARE NOTHING TO WRITE ON...creation, believe, understandin', teach, or just plain LOVE

One can't never change a page, if the light is correct...

Essence can light believe...cause is believe is essence...

Where the storm at, the sun layin' back laughin'. g'tting' ready to pour the shine...

One find truth in believe, but what side of the balance...learning in feedin' essence

Love direction is the reflection from the heart...

Quest, how is the sound of a sentence as pillar...

A tribute to a door is a smile in believe...

Silence is same in any action...

Enlightenment in one words, is a smile in sentence understanding...

Essence the universe in one words...

Grain the mile in the particle love

Words are the soil of the universe forest

Can you water the words in thirst understanding...

TEARS THE WATER-FALL OF ESSENCE

in the glass in your eyes, a smile is there...

humor is a laugh, don't waste the smile...understandin' feeder

if a words is a glass, then duct-tape is believe

BLIND IS THE EMPTY CUP...OOOPPPSS

THE CREATION OF WORDS IS LEARNING HOW TO LOOK
AT NOTHING...VISION OF VIEW

TEARS ARE DEEP IN THOUGHT, NOT IN DECISION...
AWARENESS CHOICE

LOVE IS THE HUG OF A SMILE...

a speedy mind in a slow-pace...the universe complex

a mountain the short-cut in thought...

BEFORE A DECISION
 BECAME A THOUGHT

CHAIN AND BALL CALLED A SENTENCE...

you can taste the sky
 if one thirst the stars
  the light in the dim...

the connection between two words
are the holes in the links...

The cry of print, the darken journey. The sky write it's truth in wind. Whisper in essence search ask. Deep in chemistry of nothing. Silence stand, understandin' call. Reach echoes see everything. Planted paint of art, glory gift of words. See what is seems to be saw. Carry by smile the sentence of am.

It eat in believe! But grow in thinking

Dress an emotion with LOVE, big bang myth...

Thirst for smile elegance the smile...

Experience the role of essence called TRUTH...

THE SHINE IS THE SCRIPTURE OF THE OF THE SMILE...

Break down the smile into words, so one know what the tears were sayin'...reference reflection

COVER NOTHING...

Don't judge it, just read it. The sign understanding...

keep it movin', a word can say in a smile...

there are things, examples ~ out-loud now. AND THERREE are THINGS ! ! !

define the smile in the laugh...words, words and words

Furterlisure and the soil, the present of essence. As a hug and a smile

If the sky talk to you, listen to the wind. Ask the silent tree...

If a wall rain cover your heart with a SMILE

Present the essence in everything, as believe vision the centeredness in words understanding...

In the eyes there is nothing, until the heart structure it's PILLAR...

Momery are do and don't in present in vision, guide line of the heart...

Your eyes may shine, but read it's sentence...

The game of loving is the structure SMILE...

One is everything in words...the talking mirror in HERE...

One desire for loving words, it's the smile gift...

HEAR HEARD IN AM, the looking mirror...

listen what one has to say to a words, the learning TOOL...

Silence language is quietness speaking

Kiss me to see me, ask understanding words...

A smile can be a wolf, but the sheep can become a hug...the lovin' of a word

Q smile can enlightenment any hugs...

For are the star of a smile are words...

Don't let thought decision, de-value love smile...

The area structure of words is how to combine a smile into a sentence of PROUD am

ONE CAN'T MOVE A SMILE, NOT EVEN WITH A TEAR...

PRESENT THE STARTING POINT OF EVERY-SECOND...IS AS ALWAYS

THE OPEN BOOK IS THE LOOK OF THE HEART...

THE SENTENCE OF EVERYTHING IS A SIMPLE WORD.

love is always there, just follow it's true words of am...

pouring words smiling shine...

let the emotions get wet, so they can dry out the smile...

COMPOSE A SMILE IN WORDS UNDERSTANDING...

SO IF THE WORLD CAN HANDLE ALL OF US...

SO CAN YOU HANDLE ALL THE WORDS WITH-IN...

seconds the builder of creation in a sentence...

THE IDEAL OF REALITY THESE DAYS
WHAT A WORDS AS THINKING
WHAT UNDERSTANDING TOLD THINKING

OPEN THE LENS OF SELF
THE EYES OF WORDS...

WORDS ARE THE PAPARAZZI OF SELF...

THERE ARE MANY ANSWER
OF ONE SELF THE QUESTION...

if you can answer a question, you can walk the pattern...blueprintwords

Present the light of all light. As now in a complete sentence

EXPERIENCE EXTISTANCE, walking the print...

BORN the smile, plant the words. Essence garden of ESSENCE...

Travel the experience and smile the walk...

Just, the seeker founder of I am

Love, the smile of the heart...

Essence the thinking of understanding

LIGHT, the understanding of words

UNDERSTANDING EVERYTHING IN WORDS BELIEVE...

size is not the smile or hugs, IT'S THE UNDERSTANDING WORDS

THE SKY HAS A WHISTLE IN WIND...
THE STORY TELLER OF ESSENCE AIR...

CUT THE GRASS IN WATER
TO SEE THE GARDEN IN MIRROR...
time that's all that is always...

A ROSE THE DIAMOND OF A PEARL CALLED THE SMILE

love me for I am a word
make a sentence in thought
decision the smile in BELIEVE...

mirror tellin' reflection

if one rescue a word, one done fishing...

THE CROSS THAT MAKES IS BELIEVE...

BELIEVE IS THE PAINTING PRESENT...

TODAY SIGNATURE IS SIGN BY YESTERDAY, TOMORROW PLATFORM

GIVE WHAT ONE HAS WITH-IN SMILE

THE HEART SMILE, IS THE SENTENCE WITH-IN THE WORDS...

WORDS CAN EXPLAIN EVERYTHING IN UNDERSTANDING

THE BORDER OF A SMILE IS THE HEART...

IF YOU PLANT A SMILE,
YOU WILL GROW A HUG...

thinking think...
but understanding talks...

only a hug believe a smile...

NOTHING, THE MUSTARD SEED FOR EVERYTHING...
BELIEVER OF WORDS

A POOL CAN BE LIKE THE RAIN
BUT CAN SHINE LIKE A LIGHT TOO
THE THOUGHT OF A THOUGHT

to hug a kiss, one must smile at the hug...essence understanding present the time that left are always coming, now's movement in silence...

the nutrition of ingredient are words understanding...

ONLY UNDERSTANDING PROTECT THINKING WITH ITS HAND, TO TAKE-CARE OF THE HEART

U fit into the heart as I...

only smile can dig into tears for true words...

A FOOL FOR THOUGHT...
 DON'T BUY BULLSHYT...
 IT COMES WITH UNSEEN LAIR...

PRECIOUS IS THE SMILE OF INNER WORDS UNDERSTAND-ING

TO SHINE A WORD WITH A SMILE
 ONE NEED TO HEART UNDERSTANDING

LOVE DEEP SURFACE IS THE REFLECTION IN MIRROR AS WORDS...

FOR LOVE IS GIVEN TO BECOME A MIRROR...

if one puts light in tears
 it reflects a rainbow
 the mirror of a sentence
 from the heart as SMILE...

in the journey of a sentence

words are written in chapter and scripture

path it took were shine and beauty

pillars as glory

strength as blessing

a shield as a hug

a and sword as a smile

for the one in mirror

reflects all words as one...

ONLY YOUR UNDERSTANDING SPEAK IN THINKING...SAY WHAT!!!!!!

EYES ARE EMPTY IN TEARS, BUT FULL IN SMILES...

THE LINK IN THINKING IS UNDERSTANDING AS ESSENCE PRINT WORDS

EYES THE BODY OF WORDS

UNDERSTANDING THEIR LIFE

AND THINKING, IT'S JOURNEY

PASSION, IT CAN ONLY BE GLUE BY SMILE...

AM THE ROOTS OF WORDS, UNDERSTANDING GROWTH

THE DOOR-WAY OF WORDS
AND UNDERSTANDING IS THE ONLY
THE PATH OF JOURNEY IN THINKING

DEEP CORE, CODE OF WORDS IN SMILE...

WORDS UNDERSTANDING OF MATTER IS A SMILE...

FURFILL THE MIRRORS IN WORDS

love is a sculpture in understanding, but it's not pillar in thinking

awareness focus pillars...

you can make water into soup, just smile...

MAY A REFLECTION BE IN MIRROR WORDS...

THE SMILE SHINE IS HUGS MIRROR IN WORDS OF AM...

LOVE VALUE IS RESPECT
THE ALWAYS IN HERE'S THERE

now's past and future is always PRESENT ESSENCE...

EVEN NEGATIVE WORDS PROTECT YOU, SIMPLE DON'T
BECOME THEM...THAT HOW YOU MAKE THEM POSITIVE...

THE MIRROR OF A SHINE ARE THE CORRECTED WORDS OF AM

DON'T MISS WHAT MOVE PRESENT...

THERE IS PRESENT FOR NOW...

LOVE CALL IS AM...

voices the preview in silence...

WHY CHOOSE WORDS, WHEN THE SENTENCE PREFECT...

LOVE THE SMILE THAT GROWS THE GARDEN IN WORDS...

PILLAR THE BELIEVE THAT TRUELY STANDS...

BELIEVE LOVE IN GUIDE...
LOVE THE PEN OF A SMILE...

ANY WORD YOU CAN CHOOSE AS AN UMBRELLA...

ONLY IS HERE...

nothing movement, keeper steppin'...

The rainbow around the essence call WORDS

author quietness is silence scripture...mirror thy thou thee one read the book as they ARE, silence mirror write...

SIMPLE IF YOU PICK TWO OF NONE, YOU ARE THE RIGHT
OF NOTHING...

u can look anywhere, but only has the answer of AM

the truth is in the mirror of AM

A LIGHT HANGS IN THE STREET AT NIGHT
 A WORDS BELIEVE IN A SENTENCE AS UNDERSTANDING
IN THINKING

Opposite are the same in different in understanding always mirror as is.
The there in here as reflection

For there are star called the words, for their light is understanding. As a
sentence create in believe, blessing become the I am. Self can scripture
its print. As stone is written and readin' not seen.for the thou of thee is
thee in thou...

the bit of alot
 a smile in a tears
 complex as simple
 written as believe
 one walk far in nothing
 yet conquer
 reach the bliss
 jump horizon dream
 mistaken as words

the dawn of day cry
sweet as sky
beauty as capture
essence define ebony
LOVE CENTER PORTION

FAR-BACK TOMORROW, SMILE PRESENT

Build the bridge that tears can't break, the construction site of smile

Assist words as the sponsor of it

Polishin' understanding, thinkin' will be CLEAR...

Tutor the words as understanding. A gift for a mirror

In soil there is the mirror of words

Give the blessing as understanding

FOR UNDERSTANDIN' IS THE LIGHT, thinkin' search...

Remain in the light

To walk in the step of journey, thinking must listen to understanding...

Love the smile that guide the mirror

Judgement to tear without a cry

Pillar light sculpture heart, a smile

A tear can teach the eye to READ...

GUIDE WORDS AS THE HEART...

If understanding has a scripture, why does thinkin' has an EMOtion...

As illusion is as thinking, can understanding be as BELIEVE...

YOUR FULL-NESS IN THOUGHT, COULD NEVER FIT THE NOTHING IN MY SHOE...GRAINS DESICION VS. ESSENCE UNDERSTANDING

AROUND ...I AM GOOD ...

THE DATA-BASE FOR MY SMILE
WITH THE RIBBON OF MUSIC

SKY'S AND STAR, CAN YOUR SMILE AND HUGS. MATCH IT'S BEAUTY...
SMILE AND HUGS THE MAKE-UP OF WORDS...

music it's love is a smile. and it's reach-out is a hug...

kindness caring of essence nature of love

Trade the word in a word

Be the common if there is any SENSE...

LOVE gratitude is being SELF in understanding

Love bond in self is understanding SELF...

LOVE the experience of focus AWAREness in UNderSTANDing

A MIRROR DOESN'T HAVE DIFFERENT REFLECTION...
COMPLEX WORDS

a word can balance a sentence. If they're both TRUTH

FREE IS THE SMILE GIVING TO WORDS

the candles of words, LIGHT YOUR SMILE

can you see the truth in words, called the smile...

there u are in harmony

LIFE PUZZLE ANSWER IS TO SMILE...

Living a smile reaction of love...

THE FEEDER OF WORDS...

YOU CAN WRITE WHAT LOVE IS
JUS LOOK AT THE RIGHT THOUGHT

LOVE DOOR IS THE KEY OF THE SMILE...

LOVE IS THE SHADOW OF YOUR SMILE
 READ THE SENTENCE IT HAS...

thought you might enjoy this ..;.)

i'm sendin' jw a heart wrap in muahhhhhhh

MUSIC FRAGRANCE THE SMILE...

ESSENCE THE STORY OF ALWAYS...

If life give brand, make is a SMILE

Life present is understanding muahhhh!!!

To respect smile value TEARs

MOTION IN TIME, UNDERSTANDING IN THINKING

EASY-GOING, what words say in understanding...

Suddenly you in LOVE...a QUOTE from self 2 self

Laugh appointment are SMILE...

Don't update my status, update some understanding...

Therapy, understanding...there no-place like home, there no-place like
homejijijijijiji

A SMILE IS SKILL, BY LOVE OF WORDS...

DESIGN YOUR HEART
WITH THE STROKE OF LOVE BRUSH
BY THE PICTURE SENTENCE SMILE

love only address is self...
the zip-code of understandin'...
the area-code of thinking...

LOVE Send by ESSENCE...

Mirror storm of reflection

Essence learning thinking as understanding

Kindness the grace of a sentence...

Circle the truth in a straight sentence. And that ain't square...
If you ain't I, then me is not am. Self mirror of words are reflection of
understandin' as is in here where eveythin' present...mmmm

Shame media for not cleaning mirror...

Essence the limelight of words

ONCE UPON OF TIME AS THE END...

TEARS THE GLASS OF TRUE WORDS...

DON'T LET A BLISS COVER MIRACLE...

A SMILE PAINTING ARE WORDS...

CAN ONE READ WHAT IS WRITTEN IN VISION...

A WALL IS BLIND IN AWARENESS...

THE COLORS OF THE HEART ARE SMILES AND TEARS

Foot-print the pillar of a sword...

Spell smile in words...experience

Creation, the structure of a sentence called words

Perfect the sentence written in ONE word!!!!

Complex the sentence written in the color, why the words are master piece...

NOTHING IS FILL WITH NOTHING...portion of everythin'

BTFUL IN LANGUAGE, understanding the translator of thinking

LOST MY JOB
 LOST MY WALLET
 RAINING OUTSIDE
 OHHHH, WHAT A BTFUL PRESENT I FEEL
 I AM NOT BLIND TO WORDS

JOKER WILD AT ANY JACK GAME

LOVE SHINES ANY WHERE, INDOOR OR OUTDOOR...
JUST BE THE SUN OF IT...

ONLY A SMILE CAN READ A BED-TIME STORY...

PILLAR STRONG SMILE FREELY...

HATER DON'T HAVE A SENTENCE ON THEE...

PUFF...SAID THE WORDS

PERFECT WE ARE, SIGN BY SMILE...

THE MAP FOR THE UNIVERSE IS THE HEART...
IT'S ROUTE ARE THE SMILE...
IT'S SHINE ARE THE WORDS IN LIGHT...
the tool of a smile to dry tears are words

EVOLUTION TRUTH, learning the inside of a word

love always come 1st, just look at self...

love can be sign with a smile called the hug

STRONG IS THE WEIGHT, IF CHOSEN THE WRITE FEATHERS

STILLNESS WRITES, THE PEN OF NOTHING MOVEMENT...

STAY STILL, MAKE A SENTENCE, AND THERE THE ACTION...

for the poor in no interest, giftness words shine present...

love is like a shadow, always ready for you to respond to self

understandin' back reminds how to think forward...

believe, the path way strength in words

The shorter word to represent the universe is I

SELF PAGE-ANOLOGY...

one can spell you as I in one me as self...

everything of a smile is a hug support...
there is a time upon moment called PRESENT...

the simple power of believe is understanding, thinking creation in words.
The strong in pillar vision. Nothing into everything of essence present...

the blind leadin' the blind. darkness mass with no gate...love it BRING
on the truth to break nothing wall

EVERY SECOND IS OPEN IN NOW
THE PRESENT OF ONE WORDS
VISION PATH OF A GATE

ESSENCE ENLIGHTENMENT THINKING IN

UNDERSTANDING
THE ABILITY A WORD CAN GIVE IN BELIEVE...

EVERY NOW IS THE ALWAYS HERE...

DRAW THE NOW, SHINE PRESENTS SMILE

HELP OF THE WORDS, IS SPONSOR BY SMILE...

LOVE IS EASY, WHEN SMILE GUIDE

BEGIN SELF IN WORDS...

TEST THE ANSWER OF THE QUESTION SOUND...

WALK AMONG THE WORDS...

TRIBAL LOVE IS THE CULTURE OF YOUR SMILE

A HUGS SIDE-KICK IS A SMILE...

A SMILE THE GUIDANCE OF THE HEART TRUE LECTURE
OF WORDS

love is the shine of the smile...

love packages are the proper sentence...

THE NOW OF IT WILL SHORTEN THE SECOND
a look at see finds seen... Vision view at light

pillar life form the smile...

form thinking as it create in understanding

as the air is signal by the wind, ESSENCE is signal by
UNDERSTANDING. Thinking signal by believe

I love you, said nothing to be found by everything

Essence, divine, spirit, understanding, thinking, believin', learning,
present, being, self, am, I, those are a few but the list goes etc., etc.

enlightenment the sentence of words, understand believe as essence
thinking

deep above nothing, essence understand in believe

the pages of history are essence understanding

I am the structure of essence I am words

don't measure the shoe by thought

there are wing in the wind
  the understanding story of tears
  mist essence in dryness silence

ESSENCE UNDERSTANDING BELIEVE AS VISION ANSWER
WORDS

UNDERSTANDING OF GUIDANCE IN WORDS
AS ESSENCE SOAR ITS WING,
THINKING CLEAR IT'S BELIEVE

believe, the structure in words as understanding

enlightenment believe in understanding...

I am the portion of the word called mirrors

movement a sound in words understanding

action the sentence applied to word...

A smile request is the HUG...

HEAR WHAT YOU SAY, TO GET THE CLEARANCE
ME OF ALL, THE I IN SELF

sssshhhh, just hear it...

LOVE SAID YES, WHEN NO ANSWER...

THE SIMPLE IN GIFT...

enlightenment essence appear as you look at words

love is on words, which goes your way...think for there they are

in balance half is truth to the complete story

the hidden light waiting for its call...self

LOVE SMILE IS SAID IN SENTENCE...

the weight of words are the balance sentence...

emotions are the trouble maker of words...

A tear can have a core of a tree, but understandin' know its truth

A thought can be the signature, now can the sign be the thought...
present pen

Was is a darkness of time, when present is always

Present the opportunist...
There is a light in your smile, the switch in words

Don't bluff yourself out of life, become words

LOOK FOR THE SENTENCE IN PRESENT, NOW'S WORDS

LOOK AT THE SHINE IN WORDS...

the universe the worlds vision

for I see the unknown, I AM WORDS...

ESSENCE MIRROR ARE WORDS...

DOING the IS...

LOVE VISION EVERYTHING ONES WORTH...

love is beyond a smile is the heart

essence the written of a smile

Love sponsor with thy words

everything little touch of love...

a ribbon is written in the sky, only love can vision it

east and west can be cover by dark and light...
I am faster than the turtle, and slower than the rabbit. I am time...

a song is written by love...
 a book is written by words...
 but a hug is giving by smiles...

love you as am

cry guidance are its words

essence true love is it's sentence
the crystal that hears is the heart

is reality born the smile...

wonder the bless in live

words are sign by vision...

Love the answer of question why

The accomplishment of nothing is everything...

love essence is the sentence brush...

love is given to you in words, as am the care of self...

ESSENCE SPEAK...SILENCE QUOTE
EVERYTHING GRAIN, THE MOUNTAIN THOUGHT...

DOWN ABOVE EVERYTHING CENTER IN NOTHING...

READ IS THE PILLAR
SILENCE HEARD OF SELF
THE HEAR IN HEARD

SOME SAY DON'T
EVERYTHING SAYS DONE...

ESSENCE VOLUME IS THE SMILE...

WORDS CAN ANSWER SELF QUESTION, LISTEN 2 HEAR

love surrounding sentence is self...

Love parallel is only the sentence...

The correct move is stillness movement called HEARD

a mission the sentence of a word...

I am nothing of words, that pertain to the truth. I am the believe of truth...

BTFUL IS REACH, DESIGN IN SEARCH...

I HAD A LIST OF DON'T...

one grain the copy of a mountain...

TO OPEN THOUGHTS ESSENCE
  UNWRAP THINKING DECISION

to stage a words, one must act the understanding

the part of the product that's complete of the grain...SELF

love present is the smile signed

love name is self...

love is not an image...is a blessing

love the essence written by vision

the half of love is the complete TRUTH

love begin with a smile, and end with a truth

love, to know your name, one must know self...

only love can see the mirror, a reflection that draw the heart

love only connection is understanding words...

love is the scripture of the heart...

thinking ask understanding do you love me...
understanding said why would you ask a question
that is already answer by nature will...

enlightenment the plateaus of the heart
like the valley and the stream as harmony...

when the trees and the wind communicate
a song in the air of essence...

Hugs and smiles have a HIGH volume...

If you write love in the snow, it's the signature from your HEART

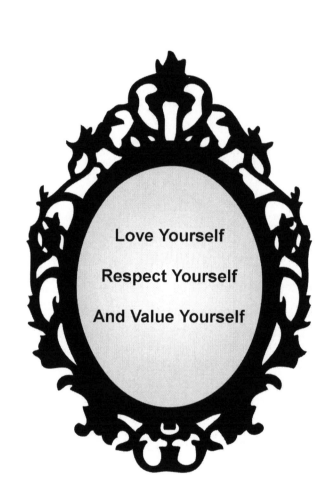

Love Yourself

Respect Yourself

And Value Yourself

Don't slip on word, you won't fall on a tear...

Love essence, the wind in the sentence

How can one be a tree, if thee the forest in the eyes of words

Stillness a mirror, the reflection is love...

Water is solid, air is free. But love is given to self, to be solid and free...

Down in nothing thought creates decision. The thinking in understanding

I can paint the picture in words, as a sentence...

Loyal words of heart...
Learn the words in a word.....not meaning only reason...

Love expresses kindness...

And spirit will...

ssshhh ask me am i, whisper said i am...

all is one
  equal is same
  everything is something nothing
  a word in essence
  is understanding thinking

a simple words makes a strong smile

words the pillar of understanding...

understanding, walk the thought in decision. how to make the thinking process...

if you put believe and action, the truth of words is born

What is essence, if not live by AM

love the smile, sign the present

sufficient of a word, the smile of a thought

Secure words in thought, makes a smile present
There is a time in always, every second of you. The I in present now

The wind sign the thought, as the decision make the air

Bless the walker in thought

Everything all is oneself

MARCH OF THE THINKER

THE HEART IN SILENCE. THE PROVEN WHISTLE

UNDERSTANDING TOLD THINKING, DON'T LET THE

WATER HIT YOU ON THE WAY-OUT...THE FUNDAMENTAL OF PRESENT

SPIRIT, THE SENTENCE IN WORDS, HOW TO CREATE TRUTH IN BELIEVING

ENLIGHTENMENT THE FOUNDATION OF INNER-WORDS UNDERSTANDING. THE AM IN ARE AS IS

ESSENCE ARE IN ARE, AS IS IN AM

LEGEND HAS IT, THAT YOU ARE

you are the I am of is, which is

NOTHING PRESENT, FOR THE LOVE OF WORDS...

do are the don't of emotion

to become, is to be...the artist of a word

only pain distance words

sculpture the sentence by defining the heart

before one talk about the reflection, look at the mirror...

Word distance, the smile

Share smile become words of heart

Love yourself the understandin' way of words

Be the words, and give it feedback...

Today is yesterday tomorrow, if you become NOW

Love action is understanding, why words help self

Love the mirror of words...

Gather the words and build a smile, essence gift

The heart is the eyes of words, understanding its sentence

ONLY YOUR HEART CAN FILL THE TRUE CUP, EVEN WHEN IT'S COMPLETELY EMPTY

WHO CAN ONE TALK TO, WHEN THERE AINT NO-MORE TREE
a kingdom can be heard, just listen to the throne...

silence action is heard...

when a quiet speak of understanding, hear the tone

understanding out-loud in silence

When is always Present
A moment is the sentence of seconds, so make the line love

revert a decision by understanding the thought...

ARE YOU FEEDING YOURSELF THE RIGHT STORY, OR THE TRUTH

DON'T SLIP ON TEARS, STAND ON SMILES...

SEARCH, THE UNDERSTANDING OF A SENTENCE AND THE ABILITY IT GIVE SELF

RELAX, LEARNNIN TO CORFORM A SMILE...

bless the founding of words in self...

gratitude the born of nurturing a word...

BLESS the forum of a SMILE

WORDS OF THE LORD, BELIEVING IN UNDERSTANDING...
AM, THE BELIEVING IN WORDS

GLORY, THE GIFT UNDERSTANDING WORDS IN BELIEVING

CHANCE IN CHANGE, THE UNDERSTANDING THE BELIEVING IN WORDS...

SPIRITUALITY THE ESSENCE IN UNDERSTANDING THINKING, AND UNDERSTANDING IS WHAT MAKE LOVE IN WORDS...

ESSENCE, THE LOVE THAT BLENDS INTO ANY WORD...

believe is the creation of words

love essence duty on moments nothing

A speech told by the heard, written the vision. And live by the words...

the truth are smiles, it was never mend to be read as tears

understanding thinking of its greeting reason

love is so peaceful, if one live in words...the I am in tribute

echoes voices is silence...

love the sun of essence, a mirror that reflects of self...

Anything, the giving of WORDS

Being there is to question WORDS

LOVE can only be surrounded by self...

Learn a new tradition, that one should turn into a culture...LOVE thy SELF
Just why it is, cause it is... mirroring self

freedom of speech, hear silence.

reality the sounds in silence words

to refill words, smile

NOT THE LAST OF TOMORROW, BUT NOT THE 1ST OF
YESTERDAY. PRESENT TIME GIVE MONENT LASTING
STORY OF A WORD.THAT UNFORGETABLE THAT'S WHAT
YOU ARE...

Blessin' words enlightenment

SEE WHAT IS SAW, BUT LOOK AT IT'S SEEN, WORDS ASKING
UNDERSTANDING IN THINKING

THE BEAUTY OF AWWW

the truth of true is the trust...

essence finest is the smile

WORDS THE SHINE IS THE REFLECT OF THE HEART...

the finest line in words is a bright smile

the secret myth of the theory is the smile, the sssshh of words

love, the trail-mark of smiles
existence is beyond the pinch...

A SECOND BRING IN THE NEW time, NOTHING CREATION

2013 IS THE SAME AS 0001, HOW TO FIX TIME... don't

walk your thought, but make sure the decision sunny

WORD IS THE ESSENCE OF LIGHT, A.K.A SMILES...

LOVE TRUE ACCESS IS A SMILE

LOVE CAN BE SHARE, WHEN WORD ARE LOOK AT 1ST

LOVE WALKS IN SMILE...

A smile is only a caring away, reach believe

What good is, when there not here...

Golden is the present, if the smile is acted...

If you wanna fill a dream make it your heart...
just cause thinking can draw, but understanding can give the real color
in believe

believing is the path
words are the doors
understanding is the key
thinking is the floor-mat
essence is the light in vision
key 2 door are words 2 understanding

SHIELDS OF PILLAR ARE WORDS OF UNDERSTANDING

THERE IS HERE ALWAYS, JUS ENLIGHTMENT...

EVERYTHING GIVEN IS THE BORN OF WORDS

THE GLASS GIVES THE WORLD TO SEE MIRROR...

FUNNY HOW THE TRUTH SOUND DIFFERENT
 BUT THE TRUTH IN BALANCE WORDS ARE TONE

STUDY SENTENCE BLESS ARE SMILE TRUTH...

BTFUL IS GIVING IN SMILE TRAIN BY THE HUGS...

THE TRAIN HEART IS THE VISION WORDS

THE RITE SMILE IS LIT, BY THE RITE UNDERSTANDING
WORDS

MOMENTS EXPERIENCE ARE UNDERSTANDING OF WORDS
LET TALK...SSSSSHHHH

perfect...ANYTHING!!!!!!!!!!!!!!

READING THE OCEAN OF THE TEARS
 WRITE THE GRAIN OF THE UNIVERSE
 THE BANG OF NOTHING
 GIVE THE THEORY OF EVERYTHING
 THOUGHTS DECISION

THINKING UNDERSTANDING
VISION ESSENCE
LOVE'S QUEST
ARE IN WORDS AS SELF

MOVING COMFORT
SMILE BELIEVE

SMILE BECAUSE YOU CREATED IT
HUG BECAUSE YOU UNDERSTANDING IT

DON'T PAINT A SENTENCE WITH WORDS
USE A SMILE AS A BRUSH...

THE HERO OF WORDS
ARE THE SENTENCE OF SMILES
HUGS BLESSING

A SMILE IS NOT TRUTH, IF IT DON'T HAVE I AM IN IT

THE I AM OF AN ECHOES, IS AM I

THE PILLAR KINGDOM IS THE WORDED THRONE...

WHY DRY A SMILE WITH TEARS
WORDS SHINE HEART TRUTH
UNDERSTANDING VISION THINKING
LOVE SIGNS MOMENT OF PRESENTS
A ROAD A PATH JOURNEY...
ONLY ARE EYES THAT HEAR...

ESSENCE ELEMENT OF MATTER
 BELIEVE IN UNDERSTANDING THINKING
 SELF I AM IN THOUGHT
 DECISION PRESENT IN WORDS

THINKING EVOLUTION WILL ALWAYS BE UNDERSTAND-
ING
 BELIEVING IN ESSENCE AS IN PRESENT...THE I AM IN SPIRIT

LANGUAGE THOUGHT DECISION IN UNDERSTANDING
 THE THINKING OF ESSENCE IN WORDS...
 VISION SILENCE IN PRESENT...

A DREAM IS HARDER THAN A WALL...
 BUT YET YOU BRAKE IT EASY...

LOVE CANT BE CURVE INTO A HEART, IF THE SMILE IS
RIGHT...

MAY THE SMILE HUG YOUR REQUEST
 WHAT IS THE MOUNTAIN
 OR THE DROP OF THE OCEAN
 TEARS OR SMILE
 OR CAN IT BE UNDERSTANDING THINKING
 THE BALANCE OF ESSENCE IN SPIRIT
 ONE CAN BUILD A WORD IN BELIEVE
 CREATION VISION IN SELF...

LOVE IS ALREADY ALWAYS

LOVE RING IS A QUIET TONE...

BRING THE HORIZON WITH A SMILE...

tears have two side...LOVE BALANCE

ENDING IN NOTHING
 NEW BEGINNING
 BLANKS FURFILLMENT

RAIN DON'T HURT, FEEDING EMOTIONS DOES...

EVEN A SMILE CAN BE WRITTEN ON BY READING

LOVE CAN REFLECT BACK, JUST SMILE

THE PATH OF A SMILES ARE ITS UNDERSTANDING WORDS

LOVE IS THE SHADOW OF YOUR WORDS CALLED
UNDERSTANDING
WHAT ONE GET WHEN ONE CROSS
 UNDERSTANDING AND WORDS
 = THINKING ACCESS IN BELIEVING=

I AM, LABEL BY A NAME...

KISSING WORDS BRING THE ABUNDANCE OF SMILES

THE BRAIN IS THE STUDENT IN THINKING
THE HEART IS THE TEACHER IN UNDERSTANDING

THE WORDS ARE THE SCRIPTURE IN BELIEVE
LOVE IS THE GRACE IN ESSENCE
CREATION IS THE BUILDER IN ACCEPTING

LOVE ESSENCE IS THE WORDS UNDERSTANDING...
THINKING ELEMENT

BUILDING LOVE IS THE CONSTRUCTION OF A SMILE...

JUST BECAUSE THERE A STORM IN YR HEAD
DON'T MEAN YR HAIR IS WET IN THE OUTSIDE

the other half is the whole episode

read between the line...as innerwords understanding

AS WORDS LISTEN, UNDERSTANDING SPOKE OF CARING

SMILE ALWAY CONQUER TEARS, CAUSE TEARS ALWAY ASK
SMILE FOR HELP...THE TEACHER OF WORDS IS
UNDERSTANDING
SIGN SMILE BY UNDERSTANDING TEARS WRITTEN...

KNOCK ON WORDS, AND WATCH SMILE ANSWER...SMILE
IS THE SECURITY OF LOVE

ESSENCE IS A SHINE, JUS ASK LOVE IT'S REFLECTION

HOME DON'T NEED FURNITURE, IT NEED SMILE...

AS ONE WALK IN WORDS
ONE SEE...
DARKNESS AND LIGHT
YES AND NO
JOY AND SAD
GOOD AND BAD
HEART EXPRESSION
BALANCE UNDERSTANDING
THINKING COMPLEX
THE FOOT-PRINT IN BELIEVE
THE I AM IN THOUGHT
THE AM I IN DECISION
OR THE GLORY OF GRACE
ONE MADE NOT DRAW A SMILE
BUT THE TEARS WILL VISION IT

WRITE OF PRESENT, READ OF HEART...

A PARTICLE OF BEAUTY, AN ESSENCE OF SHINE

TO ALL THE OPEN HEART THAT REFLECT SMILE. YOU'VE
BECOME TRUE SPONSOR OF WORDS. THE UNDERSTANDING
OF THINKING AS IT'S BEST. SILENT TALK IN VOLUME. YOU
RESPONDED IN HUGS...BLESSING ALL IN MOMENT ESSENCE
CARING

SUN-DIAL THE REFLECTION OF SMILE...

Present will always be your love, if one give it the right WORDS love will be easier, if you know why you smile

WORDS RESOLVES the guidance of understanding

ACTIVATE YOUR SMILE IN WORDS

Love will open the clear eye

Play understanding the playground of thinking

UNDERSTANDING GIVE BIRTH TO LOVE, UNDER ANY STORM, UNITY IS SHARE IN REACHING IN NEED. BLESS BE SHARE, KINDNESS BE SHARE LOVE BE CENTER

FOR EVERY-BLUE, THERE IS A LIGHT. FOR EVERY HUG, THE SMILE IS THE LIGHT...SHARIN' N CARIN' IN ESSENCE PRESENT, MIRROR REFLECT IN BALANCE UNDERSTANDING. THE AM I IN THE I AM

LOVE SHADE OF EMOTION, HAS A LIGHT SWITCH. CALLED SMILE

SCULPTURE LOVE IN SMILE...

SMILE THE ABILITY IN BELIEVE

LOVE WHAT BETTER PILLAR FOR STORM...

YOU are the time pleasure. If you are the smile present

A DOLLAR BILL DON'T HAVE VALUE, COMPARE TO THE HEART...Priceless present

YOU GOTTER BE IN IT TO WIN IT...SELF PRESENT...

YOU CAN GO NOWHERE WITHOUT SELF...

Love nothing around, every-space

LOVE IS SO EASY IN BELIEVE, JUS READ THE TRUTH WORDS IN SMILE

WHAT BETTER WAY TO LOVE WORDS BY BEING YOURSELF

NEVER BARGAIN A SMILE

A MOMENT OF LOVE IS A SENTENCE OF HUG

LOVE THE ESSENCE OF SMILES, AND THE RIBBON OF A HUG...

IF YOU WASTE A SECOND, HALF OF LIFE IS GONE. SAVE A BALANCE FOR A SMILE

MUAH SAID TO TEARS, WHY THE UMBRELLA...

EMOTION WILL TAKE YOUR TIME...

AIN'T NOTHING LUCKY, WHEN YOU DOING THE RIGHT THING. IT'S CALLED A BLESSING

WANNA SEE LOVE IN ACTION, WATCH PEOPLE DANCE. SPIRITS PRESENT

THE SUM OF EVERYTHING IS ALL, ONES PRESENT

NOTHING EVERYTHING IS MIRRORS ALL, THE SAME RE-FLECTION

LIFE IS SHORT, BUT THE DISTANCE JOURNEY IS BEAUTIFUL

PRESENT MOVEMENT OF WORDS, READ BY UNDERSTANDING...

GROWTH, THE UNDERSTANDING OF PRESENT WORDS... REBORN-THINKING

Bless for you are the walker of words, understandin' reflect essence. That you may print the signature truth of present. Smile sign now visit vision

LIFE IS LIVE BY WORDS
A JOURNEY OF TRUTH
READ BY SMILES
EXPERIENCE BY HUGS
AND SHARE BY CARING
THE CANDLE OF A CANDLE
THE LIGHT OF A LIGHT
THE I AM OF A I AM

THE SKY IS THE SMILE
THE LAND IS THE HUGS

AND LIFE IS ESSENCE

LOVE IS THE SMILE IN LIGHT...
LOVE WILL SIGN
 YOUR TIME
 YOUR HORIZON
 AND YOUR UNIVERSE
 PLUS YOUR SMILE

MY EYES WRITE, WHAT MY UNDERSTANDING READ...
WORDS VISION

GUIDANCE A STORY JOURNEY
 OF WORDS TRUTH
 BELIEVE THE PATH OF JOY
 HAPPINESS TRAVEL IN BEING
 BEAUTY IN BLESSING THE ROAD
 A MAP HAS GUIDE OF BEAUTIFUL WORDS

TIME TO START MY WORK
 BY THANKING PEOPLE
 AS THEY ENTER THEIR WORK
 SECURITY SECRET ESSENCE
 KILLIN WITH KINDNESS...LOVE IT
 GUIDANCE IS YOUR WAY
 VISION IS YOU GUIDE
 LOOK IS YOUR SEE
 BELIEVE IS YOUR WORDS

PRESENT IS YOUR WAY

LOVE IS YOUR MAP...

LIGHT HAVE COLORS, SMILES, HUGS, AND PRESENTS

MORNING TO THE WALK

BLESSING FOR ITS GUIDANCE

LIGHT HAVE COLORS, SMILES, HUGS, AND PRESENTS

WRITE A LINE OF JOY, JUST SMILE...

WORDS THAT DON'T SMILE, ARE SELFISH TO SELF...

THERE'S NO-PRICE ON WORDS

BUT UNDERSTANDING HAS VALUE

GIVE WORDS TO SELF

SEE THE VALUE YOU GIVEN

Love has an understanding, and that's you

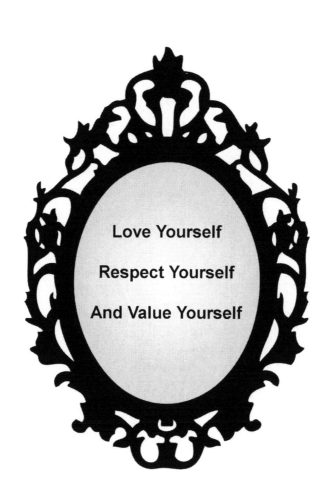

we are the doors of thinking, understanding is the key of words. essence is the shine of its belief. nothing of everything is creation of whys how. conquer, quest, search, asking tears help will replied to smile given. a view of foot-print vision, message scripture to present in one. a mirror can reflect love thirst of growth. but truth can be told in silence heard. many ears hear, but darkness silent it's hear. glory may be the page, gift will be it's words. if only thinking understand essence spirit. see the am in self is you in echoes sound heart...

THE LENGTH OF A SMILE IS THE COURAGE OF THE WORDS...

ABILITY COURAGE QUEST, BELIEVE VISION WORDS SILENT SOUND

ABILITY THE CAN IN DO...

PRESENT IS GUIDANCE
VISION PATH IN WORDS
UNDERSTANDING THINKING IN LIGHT
LOVE SEARCH OF JOY
RESPECT GLORY IN BEING
VALUE SPENT IN SMILE
SELF AM OF WILL...

OPPORTUNITY ABILITY IS BELIEVE...

present ability all's...

the lead is the thought, but remember decision can win too...

TEARS THE OTHER SIDE OF NOTHING, SMILE UN-TOLD
LIGHT

WORDS THAT DON'T SMILE, ARE SELFISH TO SELF...

THERE'S NO-PRICE ON WORDS
 BUT UNDERSTANDING HAS VALUE

GIVE WORDS TO SELF
 SEE THE VALUE YOU GIVEN

VALUE IS NO-LEVEL, ONLY THE HEART...

ESSENCE THE EYE OF THE HEART CALLED GOD...

ESSENCE CULTURE IS UNDERSTANDING...
ESSENCE WRITTEN EVERY-WHERE, BUT SEEN BY WORDS

ESSENCE THE BILLBOARD OF LIFE...

ESSENCE EVERYTHING WINDOW, SEEN BY NOTHING...

PICTURE OF A TEARS AND PURE

WHAT THE HEART CAN TELL YOU
 THE BRAIN WILL DENAIL
 AND THE EYES WILL SIGN IT AS TRUTH

WORDS PRESENT IN BELIEVE

LOVE the accomplish are words...

What love got to with it, everything nothing to see essence understanding in thinking believin' express by vision of present...

Create understanding, use the thinking tool called self...

Love has an understanding, and that's you

THE HEART THE MIND CAN THINK
 BUT UNDERSTANDING CAN HELP IT REACH IT
THE VISION IN ESSENCE HELP BELIEVE

OPEN THE HEART, BY LEARNING THE SMILE

HELP CAN BE FOUND IN TEARS, JUST LOOK FOR THE DECORATION OF A SMILE

ONLY THE HEART CAN DRAW THE SMILE, NOT EVER THE MIND...MIND MATTER

ACTION IN UNDERSTANDING IS THE SAME ACTION IN THINKING CALLED PRESENT. NOW WHICH ONE GIVE THE ACTION OF VISION

ONLY YOU CAN CONQUER YOUR SMILE
DON'T LET YOUR SMILE CONQUER YOU
YOU WILL NEVER SEE ITS TRUTH
UNDERSTANDING CAN READ ANY WORD

DIRECT WORDS TO TRUTH ASK THE SMILE...A STORY
ABOUT TEARS

TEARS WILL OPEN TRUTH BOOK OF SMILE. THE
INDICATOR IS WHY MESSAGES

LOVE IS TO GIVE YOU SMILE, NOT TEARS
 LOVE WILL BE CONTROL IN UNDERSTANDING

LOVE THE ROAD TO HAPPINESS
 BUT REMEMBER ONLY IN SELF
 CAN IT ONLY CAN BE SEEN

UNIVERSE IS AN IMAGES
 VISION IS A READER
 BELIEVE IS THE GIVER
 WORDS ARE THE PRESENT
 UNDERSTANDING IS THE ACTOR
 NOW CAN THINKING DIRECT
 PLACE WHERE ESSENCE IS IMAGE IN VISION

TIME WILL READ YOU TIME IN PRESENT
 JUST THINK UNDDERSTANDING OF NOW

BELIEVIN IN ESSENCE IS THINKING IN UNDERSTANDING...

LOVE PASSION OF TRUTH
 UNDERSTANDING QUEST
 THINKING FULFILLMENT IN WORDS

Love the image of smile

DON'T IMAGINE THE TRUTH
BELIEVE IN THE TRUTH
WORDS UNDERSTANDING CREATES

SIDE ARE TRUTH, BUT ONE SIDE IS TRUE...

BALANCE IS THE TRUTH OF WHICH SIDE ONE DECIDE
ON...

the word is born by the understanding of the sentence...creation

WHEN THE WIND IS READING
THE AIR WRITES UNDERSTANDING VISION

Give spirit a spirit, just smile. Essence will do the rest

SPACE IS THE PAGE OF NOTHING...
Want the truth, separate the word from the sentence. And become the
word from the sentence. Hissing echo
Quiet talks, it's has its own voice. The hidden language
Born to the word, whispering MIRROR
One wall told a mirror, Who am thee
Battery the water
If a sentence were to speak
It would laugh, know that the auto-correct.
DON'T SMILE CLEAR

Turn simple into a sentence

Let movement teacher action

Reflection speak
View listened
And smiles hugs
The sentence of a word

There is a reflection in the puddle sentence

There your story
There the story
In front of the
Mirror opposite
Of you which
One truly SPEAK

A HUMAN EXPERIENCE, exposing middle finger

A friend of your, is a friend on my. SAID THINKING
 tell me who you hang out with, and I tell you who you are, SAID
UNDERSTANDING
 ESSENCE MIRROR ONE AS ALL

Don't iron your tongue
Because the wrinkles are in the sentence

Going for a thirst
The patent quench

A CUP OF SENTENCE

GIVE THE TASTE OF WORD
A circle one word, paint that page

look for sound are in words called the being
as i walk in silence i am believe
vision is my page as essence
sound is my written in truth
echoes are the print of words
as wind is felt in air
vision is made in believe
thinking made be the ink
understanding is the pen
thoughts in decision are the sentence of words
as truth is read a smile is born
the story is a bessin and the glory is a gift
the theme life is simple in words of understanding

HATERS WATCHER'S MEETING, in the middle of nowhere.
Walking distance

EXISTENCE IS ONLY A WORDS MADE BY BELIEVE CALLED
EXPERIENCE...THE LOGIC OF WHAT A WORDS IS

Type like, luck will come to you. When this dollar, become a hundred
dollar BILL...

TASTE THE WATER IN WORDS, IT SHINE

The zipper of a smile are its words

Avoid hat's has shoe

About to finish 5th shift, b back later for a double lata noon

YOU ARE THE WORDS THAT ARE GIVEN
YOU ARE THR UNDERSTAND IN OF IT
YOU ARE IT SOUND
YOU ARE IT LISTEN
YOU ARE IT BELIEVE
THINK UNDERSTANDIN OF WORDS
AND SELF IS GIVEN

Sign the question
Become the second

A mirror of the word
Represent the action of the sentence

Everything in blank, smile is the author

Smile is everything, giving in any word

Study THERE, THE RESEARCH OF now

Freedom, draw it as a sentence

You can create anything, the study of blank. Hey nothing is the playground, when words are sandbox of sentence

Deep in the categories of nothing, there is something part of everything. And the example is a smile

Lying can correct, this is only a lie. Now back to your sponsor

Working seven day a week, working a double tonite. But working one swift tonite. Need to charge with some music. Been awhile some music finish with work until morn. And etc. etc. etc. etc. etc.

3 person from administration, have something against me at the embassy. Do they know I just can walk out without a sweat

The nothing accomplishments

Can you understand the language of thinking
 Only the smile can translate

The envelope bucket...

Experience can never be erased
 Skill the trade of nothing

Time the point of a sentence word

A pen can tell you the truth

PAINT ARE AS A SENTENCE

From all box sentence

There are flavoring words

The time of before and after
Erase trues present
Essence always talk in nature
As the dreams in WHY
understanding as words
Thinking as essence
Truth never been blank
For every tree of silence
For every water-related
Hearing present talk story
See for nature is in the call
Just let the eyes HEAR

Give present the opportunity to support
Understanding the format of thinking
Words of AM, creates 1 of essence

If time second become
Story can record words

Last-first, present is essence
The how now walks...

The limestone of words, the HEART

Understanding the pen of a smile

Thinking is the students
As understanding is the teacher
The blackboard jungle...

Words are present to walk in understanding, essence play-ground of thinking

Simple not hard, if it's written with its smile. THE CALLING OF A MIRROR,

A mirror has fruit, its words. Created by its sentence...

This embassy job is funny, I need permission to use the bathroom. Get this one, they gave me a walkie-talkie and I'm the only guard on duty... got love life

Gonna have some fun. Gonna play with the cup half empty, half full. How does one fill bullshyt with empty...

The patient of mountain, understanding

Study the self teacher of students
One can get more from the ground
 If the word ain't cement...

A sentence is the water, for a words growth

Don't live on the backup, one ain't got. I silver spoon for thought

The deep end of the pool, don't have water. NOW YOU CAN SWIM

For all the blessings given if they were candle, than the world is my cake...blessing at all

So much notice of nothing

Adding water to word

Time half of cup, is a decision

If money had a wallet, would it had emotions... Wait for it...

Another second blessings the words, on the podium of self

Put the image back on, the lotto is taken

won the lottery, by not buying a ticket. But still respecting the heart

Look at the view of why
 It's how, explain what

Seconds the grains of the mountains
 sentence the present of a word

Support your second of present, they are the purification of essence

BORDERS, the two-story of bullshyt

Shyt have you lost your volume, on your relief packages

Nature whose really talking for essence

Build the fortune of a smile

Sentence of a word, is the power of all

The reconstruction of words is a smile.

Why break the toy, when the smile is the key to earth...

Long day and at work to 8 morn, zzzzzz

BLESSING UPON THE SMILE

Reality present will be words

Word are not ordered with, cane, battery, or ball and chain

Cry no-mas, says the words

A teacher is a student
To teach what it's learn

Judge-Judy, remote-control

What do they have in common
A-don't judge
 B-mind your business
 C-uck off...

It ain't rocket science, it's just essence

If one anchor a word,
 It can reach the sky

A sentence in a second, it's the detailed word

The physics of word are the smile understanding sentence

I walk so far-nowhere, silence actions

The only gravity your smile has, are the one the heart shine

Take my roof, but not my house-music

Print a quest in question, outline its smile

One is not a lecture, but a smile

Words don't have string, only sentence

The mirror of sound is reflection

Speaker for any occasion, my life. House baby

Gold as smile, add it to the sentence, between the words. And watch the shine as understanding

I live in bottle
I live in powder
From the reaches of tear
The born of the smile
Pillars my strength...

Essence are believed words
As a TV screen picture
The art show its shine horizon

The drop in the oceans
The tree in the forests
The grain in the mountains
The word in the sentence
The smile in the hugs.

Gold as smile, add it to the sentence, between the words. And watch the shine as understanding
Echo speaks as reflection

Understanding, thinking spirit of the mirror

Virtual is present

The none seeing line of present

Never cover what is present

Strengths is the will in the sentence

Please battery is not included in sentences

The forest of a stream
 Is the valley of an ocean
 The color of an art as shine

The art of a word
Is the character of the sentence

Painting a sentence, as the picture word...

The rag of tears are the story to find smile

Don't put stain on tears

Thinking the mirror of understanding as pests in word

The full bucket of a empty sentence is a smile

If your heart is the blackboard
 Your smile become the billboard

Stay still while you moving, action study of present

Boom your smile with a sentence, bet the example of that word will laugh

Life is an example of nothing, created into a shine. Just ask the SUN
Understanding, the hidden answer, described as a word
If one looks at a mirror as a page, can it see the REAL time. WARNING
is not AM or PM, eastern or pacific
The he and she, please don't border the smile
The guide meter of history, always been the smile
Kindness the reach or words
Everybody is the mirror of the universe
The gift in the line of the circle is unity
The point of view present, before nothing , after nothing. The time lapse
Build the second by moment
The present is your platform, so build a sentence
Understanding is not 1 plus 1, it's about living
Mornings be the present
Truth as Present
 Master as essence

Time has no end in the line circle

When the ears decide, and the eyes are pointing. Guess what the heart is laughing.

Copy the smile of a mirror. But don't laugh just joy

ON PRESENT, call now always. Second the start of nothings everything

There is no-secret to light, just smile

Love is the sentence of the word

Repeat the word
 By dusting the sentence

Love fishing in mirror
 The bait is a word
 The catch is the sentence
 Fulfillment is light
 Understanding as present
 Thinking as thought
 Meaning as reason
 Smile as shine
 Tomorrow today
 Is yesterday's present
 A moment seconds
 As the lines circle
 Unity as the hook of tears

If view told story
 And see head-line them
 Hear become present
 As a mirror question
 Reflection answers
 Heard tell the told
 Of the tear looking
 Into the horizon

Movement as run

Action as ran
In understanding
They both mirror of one

The weight of the tear
Is the run of the ego

The fog in the tears, stop the reflection of the mirror

I carry you, said the word. Now wake up. Post the present
The new coming, learning to write a smile.

The new coming, learning to write a smile.
The basic of the sentence
That builds the structure of the word
Its reflection is the smile
Which walks amount mirrors
Understanding, the water of thinking
Just ask the tears hugging the smile

May the echo of the words
Shine the smile of reflection

Take hold of your smile, become its word. The mirror speak as a sponsor

Have you ever heard noise in the word called (FUCK-IT). Earth painted

Would you believe, the bottom of the ocean is connected to the shore...
hahahahaha had to laugh at this one

A short example, 1,000 years is like 2morro too. That's the second of a sentence

Find out why the word, got's the joke on one, hey the pearl of the silk is in words. But one is blind by the meaning not reason. If why point, now ask your self is that truth. Ssh see truth come in sound. The picture of silence, and it's has action too called present. Now hearing clearly. Can you undress the sound of the picture. Of three words walk into a bar...

Cry, the towel of a smile

Bless is the one essence Understanding
Simple as view in heard
Experience is told
One walk upon the sound
The echo of reflection
The written as say
MIRRORS THE PRESENT

47727457R00094

Made in the USA
Middletown, DE
01 September 2017